# Scottish Poetry 6

*Edited by*
George Bruce, Maurice Lindsay,
and Edwin Morgan

*for the University Press*
*Edinburgh*

# Contents

## The Old Hag. *D.M.Black*

The old hag under the signpost will not come out from the shadows.    I
tempt her with bits of biscuit—what do I know?—what is her species?—
she is unmoved at any rate.    I squat down.    The hearth is dead.    I
blow on the ash and stones.    —It's dead.    —No doubt about it.    O the
controlled
fires for cooking by are done.    (I talk to myself.)    The stomach
will not always revolt against the alternatives,
the raw, the charred.    —The live, she yells, teeth cobbled with saliva—I
swing round.    She had come forward.    She
skitters back.    Her face is invisible, under the hat's shadow.    Now,
entirely in darkness,
she gnashes and gibbers.    She is in great excitement.    I hear her clothes
rustle.

## A Poem for Peter MacCrae. *D.M.Black*

All day I brood upon my children
and kick up the dust in the road

and on their children
and on their children's children

till the future is lost to the view
of my imagination.

it is they that shall inherit the earth.
it is their dust I kick

## The Pet-shop. *D. M. Black*

Sirius my ancestor
look down upon me
I stop to say good evening to the python
the one with blond patches
he is always astir

& tonight he lies
with a pied rat in his arms;
round a loop of neck
his head ranges the soft fur of the belly
up and down
elastic black tongue
darting and vanishing;
the rat's nose is half under water
the little pink legs are rigid

he lets the rat fall
it topples slowly
in the pool another python explores it

but by one
—bent on his rock—
glides out over the water
head and neck, like a flag!
takes the rat by the muzzle
his jaws part like a suitcase
readjusts his grip

& the neck-muscles
ripple back then come surging forward
he mouths further

his neck distends
like a stocking!

the coils of muscle
retire pause and come forward
he sways slowly
the rat moves over the pool
he makes a trifling advance
—all-but sticks at the shoulders—
nothing deters him
ten inches of him are in spasm

the mouth advances

past the forefeet he goes steadily
the fat white belly
enters his head–like–a–heart

by the fifteenth minute
hindfeet and tail
hang from his jaws
he rests without passion

he swallows them down
and the rings of muscle contract
and the rat travels
—great bulge in the slack morocco—
some ten or twelve inches
there comes to a halt

& the jaws so atrociously parted
renew their acquaintance
they yawn and snap
he lets the tongue loll
black flickering fork from a pink plinth

& the head journeys
restlessly over the pebbles, along the glass
about his own folds

I go from the window
it is midnight, cold, and the streets are unsafe
Sirius lead me


**Syllabic Sequence.** *Alan Bold*

it was at five the meeting i knew the
others were frightened but had decided
to go through with it whatever the con
sequences it was raining when we met
and we ran over the plans huddled in
an alleyway i was to drive they said
the others would follow me with the prize
it was colder and i felt afraid the
others wiped the moisture from their brows and
started to move was it the rain or the
sweat provoked by fear i didnt know i
kicked the ground and started to walk away
from them that was the thing to do i thought
separate keep a distance no prowling
guardian would suspect the sun was dull like
a lamp seen through frosted glass mist was dipp
ing over us almost six now four hours
to wait i could not drive around the place
for ever i was too conspicuous
i waited for darkness but my eyes per
petually adjusted to the change
of tone and i became confused about
the time i could hardly concentrate just
sitting there inside it was too warm to

keep endlessly alert i had to change
our roles i should be the one seeking the
prize one of the others must be inside
the warmth waiting for me bells started to
bang almost immediately after the
job started the prize was within our reach
glittering and liquid like the suns re
flection on a lake every time i heard
the wind i thought it was a guardians whine
every time a dustbin clattered in the
wind i thought it meant the ubiquitous
gong every time i heard a voice i thought
it must be the voice from the other side
when the bells started to bang i told my
self to ignore them they were battering
out my own fear while the prize was within
our reach there was no fear we had agreed
on that to see it blindingly bright a
short distance from us outshining our lamps
pressed us forward the prize resisted the
hands of the first but i managed to with
stand the heat and held it tightly in my
fist o my fingers tingled and then burned
but to have the prize in my fist was won
derful i was now oblivious to
the bells and unaware of heavy in
sistent footsteps clattering around us i
held on as brutal fingers wrenched it from
me bent me from it i remember watch
ing it receding then a pounding as
if someone had put me inside the prize
my vision became red and blurred the prize
flickered out in front of me i opened
my eyes but could see nothing i tried to
move my fingers to touch but my body
refused to respond i blinked trying to

see something but discerned only a smell
of dampness now my body was beginn
ing to stir it was in pain but seemed a
part o i remembered the prize wanted
to know where it had gone where did you take
it i shouted silence i want to see
it again just the nauseating stench  ..
of swampdamp no indication of space
or time i would have to crawl the first thing
i came in contact with was a wall two
feet or so from where i had woken up
i touched it with my hands feeling a quick
surge of shocking pain as i did so then
pushed out my legs as well i could they too
touched a wall i was in the hands of the
guardians what did it mean to have glimpsed the
prize to have held it in my hands and then
relinquished it for memory is no
substitute for complete control


## We. *Alan Bold*

We shall dewdrench our faces
in the long greengrass on a cool
morning in spring and then laugh
at the blue interrupted by white spaces
in the sky.   We shall be still
only if the colours do not please enough:

because we have come suncrazed not to listen
to the eloquent advice of the frowning rocks
but to forget everything but touchtasteseefeel.
So we expect our lips to taste the mist in
the air and relish it.   We want our walks
to be open trusting everything that is real:

because we are sick of explanations and
fed up being merely human.   We would prefer
to investigate the tingle of the senses
unprocessed by precedent.   Farewell the bland
models of the past, farewell the despair
of being smart.   Welcome unaccusing glances.


**Honeysuckle all over a Tree.** *Derek Bowman*
*The honeysuckle coils in terror.* Annette von Droste-Hülshoff

Some call it parasitical
—Rambling and straggling all over
Some tree it happens to have set
Its heart on.   But I can't help feeling
It's not greedy, rather frightened
To death.   Can't you see it clambering
Up all over branches, running
In and out in panic between
The foliage, swaying and hanging
On somehow in this wind, trying
Somehow to get and keep a hold
On things?
            But what bold trumpet-blasts
Of life fulfilled it shall send forth
Into the sun-light when at last
It clusters with flowers, and what scents
Melting the evening-leaves it cleaves
To still so very precariously.

Now all for weeks it can manage
Is to sidle shoots along, curling
The parent-branch without the suck,

The clutch of ivy that seizes
The trunk . . .

                    O feel, feel these tendrils
Of fear, frantic tricks of poetry,
Of longing for the truth—the tree of life.


**Bird in a Thaw.** *Derek Bowman*

I saw a blackbird on a half-frozen lake
Step lightly, daintily so as not to pierce
The wafer of ice left a bird to trip on.

Step my bird. Step, flip! hey! through!—quick!
Prick up your tiny claw, don't slip through
The ice: the water's black and deep and cold
And your life's warm, and that tiny heart
Beating, beat, beat, oh! don't get cold and wet!

I thought that's the way to walk out life.
Skip the deeps.   It's drear down there.   No good.
Especially not for a bird, who, holy Augustine says,
Has no soul, so must make his Heaven here.

### Nine Poems of Rognvald Kolson, Earl of Orkney *(c. 1099-1154)*
*George Mackay Brown*

1. *The young Norwegian, nephew of Saint Magnus, lists his accomplishments some time before he became an Earl in the west.*

Chessboard, tiltyard, boudoir
Know my sweet passes.
Old writings are no mystery to me
Nor any modern book.
Skies flash in the snow,
Arrow flies, oar bends,
Harp cries under ritual mouth.
At the red forge
My clamorous shadow is sometimes rooted.

2. *When he was fifteen, Kali—not yet called Rognvald— sailed on a merchant ship to England. This poem comes out of homesickness, on the slow heavy bargaining of the markets.*

Five weeks our keel was choked
In Grimsby mudflats.
Water and earth rotted, a fermentation
Of foul gray honey.
Unfurl, white sail,
Eastward, over the loose waves,
A wild free skua
To the hand rack of Bergen.

3. *The Earl's two ships, Orkney-bound from Norway, were wrecked on Shetland in 1148. He recited a poem in a farm where they found shelter.*

*Help* and *Arrow*, those slender seekers,
Scatter to a hundred boards.
Women will weep for this.
Men will go with hard lips.
Poet and storyteller
Should be glad of the shipwreck many a winter night.
The sailors too
Will ravel their skill with a tougher thread.

4. *The farmer's wife that same night brought a skin cloak to the Earl, and got a poem in return.*

In a princely coat, stiff with dragons,
I leapt from the wreck,
Cold now, sea-insulted,
I stand at a Shetland fire.
With tattered sealskin
The women cancel my nakedness.

5. *Twelve of the shipwrecked men were quartered on a farmer in Gulberwick. But Einar refused to receive them unless the Earl was also his guest.*

Einar, laird, though at your board
You give room to no stranger
Except the chief stranger came, the Earl,
Yet set out horns
And ring your hearth with benches.
Tonight I am riding
To visit your unpopular house.

6. *The Earl, returning from the creels and lines, stumbled on
a sea bank with his fish. A woman laughed, thinking he
was a poor fisherman. He made this poem then.*

Fisherman, what profit today
From your net and hook?
   *Beaching the boat, arse over eye in seaweed,*
   *I caught sweet mockery.*
Fisherman, up with your cowl.
Show the silk hag
A sea lord, commander of ships.

7. *The Earl studied, one Yule-morning, a tapestry on the
wall of his palace in Orkney. The figures in the web
seemed to suggest that evil and ugliness and cunning would
in the end overcome simple honesty. He shuddered
perhaps with a foretaste of his own death.*

Two figures, one a dwarf
Burdened with hump and sword
But sewn in gold, a glittering toad,
The other a tough experienced skipper—
In this lordly web
They dance together, fixed and futureless.
Will hunchback pierce here?
That is a witch's question.
Their swords go quiet as fish through the linen silence.

8. *That same Christmas the Earl was violently attacked by a madman.*

Verse is a golden ring, a gathered silence.
Nobility a cloak, quartered.
Heroism a rune, cold cuttings on stone.
To-day on the claw of frenzy
I fluttered, a naked soul.
In a shower of masks and screamings.

9. *In the French port of Narbonne, on pilgrimage to Jerusalem, the Earl fell in love with Ermengarde. This is the first of many lyrics he made for her.*

The hair of the woman
Is long, a bright waterfall.
She moves through the warriors
Rich and tall as starlight.
What can I offer for this?
A red claw,
A cold vagrant eye.


## Honeysuckle. *George Bruce*

Honeysuckle grew at the back door
of the house sheltered from the salt
wind by the granite wall.   Girls came
to kiss there by the washing green
and the honeysuckle blossoming
while the sky was falling into night.

Under an impeccable noon sky
father left by the front door,
shoes shining, moustache bristling,
navy blue suit without a spot,
to do business, with a view to
profit, to keep the house upright.

At the back door the stars
reeled about in a purple sky,
drunk on honeysuckle dew.
Into a night of small noises,
voices one to another—lovers.
The back door squeaks shut.

## Paula's Wedding Presents. *George Bruce*
*Spring 1971*

The chestnut has begun to bud.
The children play with skipping ropes
in the street.   They run up and down
the pavement shouting.   A boy in a red
jersey draws two pistols and shoots
all the Indians that we are.   Everything
is very traditional.

The teenagers are doing their best
to show they are different from their parents.
Boys grow their hair to their shoulders,
girls have coats that pick up dust
from the road—or show their
legs to the hips, or wear dull blue jeans.
Whatever happens they must shake off
the 'corrupt bourgeois society of their fathers.'

In the Spring evening we go to see
Paula's presents.   An odd thing has come about.
All the kitchen-ware, pans, pails, bowls,
cups, saucers, jugs, pots, coffee-pots,
table cloths, tea cloths, dish cloths, mops,
serving dishes, containers of every kind,
have become splendid.   Each cup shines
with the knowledge it will contain
first love.

Everyone talks in the house.   The objects
have their stillness, waiting for us
to go away, to become themselves.

# Chestnut Tree—June 1970. *George Bruce*

This year the candles came late.
Waiting for June they burned in the sun.
At night they lit the moon that lit
the destroyed graves of the children of Peru.

Candles—do you burn with hate or love
or with nothing at all?   The priests
lit candles for the dead of Peru
walking into the ruined night for love.

The candles, erect on the plangent leafage,
dance a ritual dance in the Scottish wind.
They incite the children to tumble.
to ride their bicycles without hands,

to ridicule an old man passing by,
to swing on the plunging branches in the wind.
The children shout for joy.
They disappear into the body of the tree.

At night the tree is a torch.
Its bare branches are ash.
A bird flies into the sky.

## Catch. *George Bruce*

*For Alexander Scott on his return from Greece, loaded.*

You, Alex., went to the Aegean,
came home with a shining shot,
clean, unmarked fish.

I shot my nets thirty miles
East of North off Kinnaird,
came home with spents,

the rest torn bellies.
The dogs had got them.
Too late in the season.

That's what legends do,
purify the seas.
They're in short supply here.


## President Nixon Announces the US Invasion of Cambodia on TV. *Tom Buchan*

Spokesman for the White House dadaists Richard
M Nixon reads from his desk a 5
year old laboriously spelling out words
he doesn't rightly understand

his singsong voice gropes up
and down 'with reference to Goldilocks and the 3
bears I have decided . . .' and he lets a petrified look
crash on his script to discover the beginning

of what he has decided mispronounces it
drops a sincere octave and one
syllable which he fumbles for trips over
gawps at grabs and replaces in the sawn-off word

finally reassembled as 'excisively . . .
exluse . . . ex . . . exclusively . . .' his shaky finger tracing
the words on his wad his plasterboard hand beating out
the emphases in precisely the wrong places

his face built up with mortician's wax
somewhere behind the cameras
his dead mom Pat his shrink
and the teleprompt girl having the shits

as mr richard m nixon MR PRESIDENT
announces the US invasion of Cambodia
(Cam-bod-ia) on TV and sincerely his sincere right eye
fixes the poor old silent US majority

with Operation Total Myopic Solemnity
while its shrunken partner independently
scurries about in its socket
waveringly rolls right up searching around up there

in his poor old silent Californian grapefruit
for the next syll—
able while the right eye continues to commune
with itself in a moment of awful suspender

it will never regret eventually remembering to remember
its script and painfully
lassoing the next unfortunate phoneme waiting
to be recognised spelled out mispronounced

or whatever—CUT to mr president at the Pentagon
being briefed mobbed congratulated
comparing analphabetically but favourably
the boys out there in the Parrot's Beak and the Fish Hook

with them bums burning the campuseses
and then via satellite we are treated all over again
to misterpresident of the US leaving the Pentagon
unleasing his dentures on fat-arsed Pentagon proles

his deadpan dewlaps
anxious shuddering decisive and catatonic
all at the same time surrounded by his middleaged
aides advisers security men secretaries generals

and his impregnable cerebral armour
when suddenly a reporter opens fire with a QUESTION
'Mister President . . .' and mister president shuts up
zips up folds up turns round fumbles bales out decamps

and RUNS while back on the videotape
his boys roll back Cambodia
(CAM 2 on the accompanying inaccurate
diagrammatic sketchmap) with fire and blood.

Meanwhile (dateline moss-cow) Comrade Leonid
Nebuchadnezzar Brezhnev in a weird soft hat
reviews the latest lumpen May Day parade
with a stiff diminutive wave
reminiscent of our own dear Queen and turns
cranking his rusty mouthpiece open
to extrude a few dried vocables
at his mummified sidekick Kosygin.

And as if that wasn't enough
we next have ex-President Lyndon Baines Johnson
well-hung as a superannuated Texas bull

interviewed by Walter Cronkite
          as to his personal recollections of that day in Dallas
he was sworn in to the presidency

genitals stuffed down his left trouserleg
he recalls that Mis' Kennedy (always the fashion plate)
was wearing 'a nicely pressed pink garment'

m' relations with Jackie on Air Force One
how some of the Kennedy men let m' down
what Bobby said how ah drafted Earl Warren
rewriting history with the pendulant ex-presidential penis
vast reflatable balls
bulging his old man's pants.

Cut to MISTER richard PRESIDENT m
nixon announcing all over again

that Goldilocks and her three bears
have decided to invade Cambodia

and bring the boys back home
who at this very moment are marching on.

## Ulysses. *Tom Buchan*

Nailed to the prow of my clinkered boat
beneath me fathoms of utterly inimical water
and worlds away on the horizon
the low line of uninhabited islands

a weird wind chills the skeleton inside me
raising the weary skin on my cracked hands
whimpering the grey hairs on my skull

thinking for once of strong men
my companions now dead and totally
incommunicado

of my far-off alien possessions
my wife and children
so counter to me and separate

my cold passionate blood lives in this senseless wind
and my heart beats with a calm
beyond sex beyond sleep beyond death beyond
even my old idiosyncrasies.

**To my Father.** *Stewart Conn*

One of my earliest memories (remember
Those Capone hats, the polka-dot ties)
Is of the late '30s: posing
With yourself and grandfather before
The park railings; me dribbling
Ice-cream, you so spick and smiling
The congregation never imagined
How little you made.   Three generations,
In the palm of a hand.   A year later
Grandfather died; war was declared.

In '42 we motored to Kilmarnock
In Alec Martin's Terraplane Hudson.
We found a pond, and six goldfish
Blurred under ice.   They survived
That winter, but a gull got them in the end.
Each year we picnicked on the lawn;
Mother crooked her finger
As she sipped her lime.   When
They carried you out on a stretcher
She knew you'd never preach again.

Since you retired, we've seen more
Of each other.   Yet I spend this forenoon
Typing, to bring you closer—when
We could have been together.   Part of what
I dread is that clear mind nodding
Before its flickering screen.   If we come
Tonight, there will be the added irony
Of proving my visit isn't out of duty,
When (to myself) I doubt the dignity
Of a love comprising so much guilt and pity.

**Three poems/one poem.** *Scott Eden*

*I*

Some mockeries
I can't quite gather, like
the falsity with which I
recommend the grace I find
in gales, the falsity with which
I comment on the tabernacle nature
of the trees:

as meaningful
to insult the feather
on the buzzard, demand
the otter's license
to footprint the silt,
convict the clouds.

For these are places
we may not
participate; such flatteries
as mine
do not inhabit
their vitality.

*II*

I know why man may not
be memorable:
glib poetry's not so grand
as feeding sparrows, watching
how they give not gratitude,
but turn again to preen
or find the flea.   Such purpose
at my very window
makes me shudder at how many ancestors
have been
who could have shown these songs
for beggar's moans, but held instead
to perfect speechlessness.
How many saints
did we not count, forgetting
that the perfect sage
goes quite unnoticed,
asking only alms.

*III*

We are composed
of skeleton and sentiment
and something else, a lack
by which we stand inelegant
upon our own two feet

and know no geography,
no anthropology: our special subtlety
has shaved us to pathetic animals
that have no language
and no jubilees, but only
confrontations, blatant instances
of god addressing god
through dull opinion's screens
of disencouragement.

The skeleton subsides, the sentiment
persists; and still I swear
the snow falls not by any chemistry,
but out of love, to overwhelm
the blisters on the earth
in delicate celestial celebration.

**Stroking swans.** *Scott Eden*

swans
at tarbet
sunset
swansdown soft
soft as sherbet
down at tarbet
at sundown, swans
set down
softly on the water
by the settling sun
wafted
on the water / swans
down in the
low water tarbet sunset / whiter

than the bread we fed them.

### Cirrus. *Scott Eden*

My climate's attributes include
the high scraped cirrus congregations
taking part across the sky
these russet days.   (And south,
the hanging haze
over discordant, unsubstantial cities.)
So I choose
this place; the typical uneasy me
that goes to the bone to find air, finds
this crystal atmosphere contributes details
for the feeding of my
extraordinary greed.
    I'm infiltrated by the air,
I clutch the random vapour sculptures
from their altitudes
and warp them to
the credentials of my imagination.

My most amazement
is the clouds' continuing ceremony; I know
that something benefits
from how no slight remark
determines them, how they remain
remarkable, suspended
in their cool colossal vagueness.   Yet
they make no sound that does not
interfere with
us; they freeze and fade
alternately and unintentionally,
like the pulses
in our spasm hearts.   But we
are windswept by comparison.

Think then
on their forays and their
forays' gaiety, and on
their gaiety's integrity: and let me be deliberate,
and simulate them
in their bright unbridled carelessness.   And
let me form myself meticulous
as they, let me be undisturbed to watch
the cirrus weave the sky, a tapestry
of particles
that overruns the blue
in gentle anarchy, leaving
no sullen stain,
playing no masquerade.

I'll watch them
till that chill simplicity
obliterates my disbelief.   My body
lifts its eyes unthinkingly
to see the cirrus at the sky, and claim
its birthright therapy—the immeasurable calm influence
of perfect balanced energy.

Cold ice in the high air:
to be administered
when the heart abhors.

## The Cauld Lad. *Jake Flower*

Gilsand Castle is his hame
Who houthers there for loon or dame.
His kipper-kaper gait is skeich,
His skiddie-look is lifetimes auld,
His claichin' yap is droll an' dreich.
These een freeze lovers first, then stare:
   '*Cauld, cauld, aye, cauld.*
   *An ye'se be cauld for evermair.*'

When still an unforbidden lad,
His gezling uncle left him clad
In naething, and the tacket deed
   Chitterin' curses on the bauld
Baurdy batchie who had need
O' houghmagandie past his care:
   '*Cauld, cauld, aye, cauld.*
   *An ye'se be cauld for evermair.*'

Ye ken noo if a'body's set
For death if by the deighle met.
Still shiverin', drony and fore-done
(Like lambs o' winter in the fauld)
He stalks the lusty—anyone
Who daurs to dae whit warns the air:
   '*Cauld, cauld, aye, cauld.*
   *An ye'se be cauld for evermair.*'

## What Will Ye Wear? *Jake Flower*

What will ye wear to my tombstone, lass
What will ye wear?
  *Babbs on my belly, man*
  *Sneed on my locks,*
  *An' eat*
  *A carnock-pear.*

An' will ye tak tae faedom, lass,
An' fin' a man?
  *I've got your parrymak*
  *Seven years from now*
  *Whae ends*
  *What you began.*

## Symie's Song. *Jake Flower*

Symie is a gey braw blether
  Het rows and butter-bakes
Likes tae be a hide-i'-the-heather
  Het rows and butter-bakes.

Symie moves sae hiddlinwise
  Het rows and butter-bakes
Ye can't see him when he cries
  Het rows and butter-bakes.

  *He's a fell dram-hearted fella*
  *Greets fur mortals, one an' a',*
  *Sae wid you, Jock, and you, Stella,*
  *Eftir sich a busteous fa'.*

Hae a gustfu' life then, a' yis,
   Het rows and butter-bakes
Soon will symie want tae ca' yis
   Het rows and butter-bakes.

## The Auld Symie. *Jake Flower*

Winter is deasie
   An' ootside the snaw
Churns like a salmon
   In its daid-thraw.

White gettin' mair white
   Piled on the stanes
Folk look stark naked
   Clad in their banes.

But still the auld symie
   Wi' bent kipper-nose
Maks for the kirk where
   God alane goes.

## Hielan'-man's Funeral. *Jake Flower*

This guergous hielan'-man may look
   A killer in his kilt.
Howananbee, this hoose-side hates
   Tae see the fell bluid spilt.

He kipples up wi' air an' birds,
   An' if he sees ye shoot
The sand-lark or the crane-swallow
   You'll feel his buckled boot.

## Three Underwater Poems. *Robin Fulton*

1

what happens to the intolerable space?
we stand here at an unmeasured depth
with wine glasses, overshadowed by flowers
I imagine the surface of the night sky

'the history of broken things' he says smiling
and I remember the beautiful crystal spheres
that somehow survived the minds dreaming them:
the reflections, the curved fragments survived also

'coming home again' she says 'I watch
the lonely waves unfold in the city streets
I touch a flower, it tears my hand like coral
our words merge as blood whines in our ears

*La Cathédrale engloutie* next door,
from our own lit windows dance music
and sudden laughter like glass breaking, we grope
across the lawn like shadows on the ocean floor

2

what happens to the intolerable weight?
as if flesh became spirit yet was still
flesh, we stand in a giant glass bubble
on the ocean floor, our ears stop whining

instead 'Mahogany Hall Blues' you cry
I say 'Louisss—you blew that note
five years before I was born'
forty years on and glowing still

(survived like a china cup in an air-raid)
what happens to the intolerable time?
here it is too deep to flow, it weighs
on the incredibly thin glass of our dream

*rapture of the deep :* those outside
stare in with distorting faces
we can see straight through the drained eyes
of those who are for ever on the point of dissolving

3

the history of sunk things, the divers roll
weightless in clear water before descending,
out of the sun's reach they will remember
a sphere of intolerable brightness

deep enough down in our own element
our element is too much for us, our hearts
race, the music we imagine slows down
as we count survival out by the second

bright coral grows on the broken ships
the all-clear has wailed for a generation
but down here our ears stop whining
as we yield to the intolerable weight

*nitrogen narcosis* of the spirit:
the rainbow shoals, the transparencies
swirl for ever before the eye-sockets
through which the darkness on the other side stares

## from In Memoriam Antonius Block. *Robin Fulton*

3
the tree   whose green light you praised all
summer
is now
black and infinitely complex against
burnished
pale skies,
hardening in their own time its branches
are as now devious   snaky   crookt

your imagination has gold borders   you turn
idly page
by page
the giant picture book The Rise and Fall
of the Tree of Life   the bark wrinkles   rust
beautifies
fall
each plate shows humanity's
archetypal pose   listening

your imagination also has black borders
season by season it is never quite untrue
as now
you read
'once a man was sitting under a tree'
and the words are true   you are still sitting there
listening
the voice
now is human neither owl nor
the arthritic creak of wood   now
the voice rustles   an incessant whispering
'these were our orders, our orders!'

there is no anguish in the voice    you can't reply
the black borders are a stain spreading inwards
this picture will soon be a pinpoint

4

the eye widens
dark grey becomes light grey
what is there for the eye to see?
an aerial whispers 'they're back' — hell-fire
can be avoided at the correct angle
and now someone is boasting: 'if I could break
clean out of your atmosphere
would you scorch me up at re-entry?'

now all of us wake, the eye is red
trees are red also with blue shadows
is there more now for the eye to see?
an aerial whispers 'apple-bright' — did
the first apple bite at the first apple surprise,
the inside like packed snow not
spilling red?    an ideal that hovers
out of reach and survives its own burning

the eye narrows
red and blue become dark grey
what was there for the eye to see?
an aerial whispers 'pre-industrial,
our feelings'    boasting was finished early
and we have worn ourselves all out
at the heavy wooden devices our fathers used
these are our life though they wear our lives away

the eye closes
we nurse the flame that could up and curl all

5

the great emptiness between Merak and Dubhe
belongs neither to Merak nor to Dubhe

we are deceived by day   our eyes shimmer
widen   cloud over with a blue mist

we bask under a giant tree   we point
at flowers within reach along the horizon

we are clairvoyant, hypersensitive:
a pinpoint of light is a distant train
growing smaller and smaller with someone waving
—we forget who it was we parted from

towards nightfall our eyes clear
the blue mist of innocence thins away
the outer darkness opens   eyes glint

now peering through screens of foliage
becoming transparent and invisible

'the outer darkness'   we repeat the phrase and point
then hesitate as ripple after ripple
widens out   the curves fade and break
the ripples widen inwards mercilessly

Merak and Dubhe are pinpoints   they flicker
on a moist light-sensitive membrane
the great emptiness between them is not theirs

## Perfect. *Robert Garioch*

I'm daft.   They say I'm daft, and they're richt!
Lissun afore I speak.
I like to turn out a bit of wark that is perfect,
or raither would be perfect,
if only the customer had perfect patience.

I like to mak, say, a table out of a tree,
That table maun be perfectly flat and smooth.
I maun see my face in it.
Ken what I mean?—see my face perfect,
no blurred or twisty-ways, not wan iota!

When I say a tree, of course, I mean some boards—
I'm no Robinson Crusoe!
Wood is sweirt.   It's no willing.
It's naitur is to haud up a lot of leaves, and swas about in the wind.

Wood doesnae want to be flat.
It wants to rax itsel and twist about.
I choose timmer, that auld and seasont,
that muckle droukit and dried and blaffert about,
it has lost aa ambition to dae as it likes.

Wood doesnae want to be smooth.
I place it and sand it and try it
on a deid-flat surface.
I sand it and try it and sand it finer.
And when I'm finished, I dae it again.

Wood wants to stay the colour it started.
I stain it wi dragon's blood or turmeric,
burnt sienna, Fernambuco wood, burnt umber,
Indigo, even, if I'm in the mood.

Wood wants to be rauch and grainy.
I rub in filling, and sand it finer and finer.
Thair again, raw linseed yle and shellac in spirits
are sweirt to mix.   I mix them.
And thair's yir polish.   Or anither wey,
byled linseed yle and pouthert tripoli,
and two days' wark—thon's better still.
Polish daft, I am, polish without end,
puily-pouther, pumice, crocus, jewellers' rouge,
and every job sent out afore it's duin,
naething-like perfect yet.

I ken I'm daft.
I wark wi naitur against naitur.

But aa that is in fact a thing of the past,
I hae been moved wi the times.
I'm in chairge of a machine as big as our hous.
I set the pynters on the dials, press a button;
out comes, say, Honduras mahogany, shade nine.
I dinnae ken hou it got thair.
I dinnae ken what it's made of.
But it's perfect, perfect,
perfect every time, and I dinnae like it.

It's daft I am, no aathegither donnart.

## Self Transcendence. *Duncan Glen*

we set up gemms
   for wee boys to play
Tom agin Billy
   or better
team blue agin
   team red

maks it mair sportin
   mair interestin

we caa it education

but soon
   we are grown up
put childish weys
   ahint us

we hae naething personal
   in it
its greater than oorsels

we juist blast them aff the grun
and caa it
liberation


## Bacchae in Suburbia. *Duncan Glen*

You are feart, son?

Hae I seen your mither?
She's settin up the wine
song and dance?

You are feart, son?

King Pentheus sits on his throne
and the Queen's gane huntin?

You are feart the lions are
waitin?   See her as hersel?
Your mither?

You *are* feart, son?

She'll hae you by the hair?
On a plate?   Your mither?

You *are* feart, son.
She's settin up the wine
song and dance?

Hae you lost your heid, son?
                              Or waur?
                                    Son?


## A Journey. *Giles Gordon*

Stepping out from the village, stepping eastwards
—two miles, three miles, ten miles—across three bridges,
up and down two hills, past one well-kept graveyard.
'Fine evening', says an old man, clipping a hedge.
It is not raining.   Now it begins to rain.
You walk on and on, until you reach a field.
You stand in it, hear the sounds of animals,
the cries of birds, the hums of insects, the noise
of a car's engine (though you do not know where).
The village becomes town becomes city.   You
admire a daisy, blow a dandelion clock.

The twenty cows all face the same direction,
eat at the same angle as one another.
Suddenly they disappear through the green slope,
the field on which a moment ago they grazed.
Rain and mist have reduced visibility
to the length of your shadow.   There being no sun
there is no shadow.   You look down at your legs:
your thighs are there, but not your feet.   You look up:
nothing to see.   You look down again: your chest
is there, but nothing below.   You look around.
Your eyes search for someone, for something.   There is
no space, no time, no landscape, no-one, nothing.

**from The Irascible Poet.** *Andrew Greig*

1) Himself

The title is, of course, his own affectation;
wayward and incalculable, yes,
but he lives easily in his body,
his own ideal.

A sociable retreat.   An evening caller
will find him an excellent host;
any subject deserves his full attention
till, tiring, he'll take up a book.

The world can keep its problems,
he has his own—the vagaries of weather,
his stubborn Landrover, potato blight.
Selfish?   He remembers it's your body
you die of, and does no harm.

Thus himself: poet & crofter & master
of neither.   But what matter?
Plenty of advice on farming
and Life's the best poem.

2) Marry the lass?

Body black in the rock spine of Quinag
the thought intrudes: marry the lass?

Easy to spend a lifetime
with the minimum of fuss and many sunny days . . .

He dismisses the thought, and the day
is spent struggling with unyielding rock.

Through evening the return is made,
fingers loose, grey eyes on the far Atlantic—

Also recalling her mother's ballooning outlines.
Home again.   The piratical poet

Decides they will instead enjoy the
fashionable fruit of living in sin,

And muttering defiantly 'Many good years yet',
takes his boots off, has a dram, forgets the matter.

4) Collecting things

The Irascible Poet has recently been collecting
anything that crosses his path: postcards
of the moon, broken fiddle strings,
a fisherman's boot (yellow), and assorted
Squeezy bottles.   His fertile mind

has already invented
a dozen things they are no use for.
Today—a fortnight after her
last note—he loaded the lot in
his boat, and loosed them to the sea,
and turned for land.
Tomorrow he will have to find a new way
to fill that empty space

5) His Own Explanation

My life is the true dream, lived
near the land, hard by the sky.   What is
needs no elucidation.
My poetry is a plan for saying
'I love you' (usually), 'Past is gone'
or 'I dig a pony'.   No magic here,
but a certain effectiveness
that pleases Man's ingenious heart,
and sometimes his soul.
I would be content indeed to see
poetry supersede prose, as the crossbow the cudgel.


**The Worry-Beads.** *Andrew Greig*

These beads: thirteen on a gold string;
                  sea pears
        ripened on Aegean beaches,
plucked by thoughtless fingers
swing and clack, finely unbalanced
                  instruments of precision

After work or in tavernas,
what clicking and squeezing the jade nipples

as we flex our wit
    over the price of bread and life
and debate inwardly—for lips say one thing,
beads another, as across Greece
    they shuttle from dawn till dawn
in open-ended prophecies.

Returning, I sold my wine
to a South African homosexual
but kept the beads—and kept
my fingers from evil, politely refusing
    a shower together.

I had thought to keep them always,
but in this town of Knox & Maxwell
they seem to be gone, now.

Evening now.   He is sitting
   looking out.   The late sun draws out
   a huge forehead, supple, oiled,
like the finely balanced instrument
   behind it.   Shadows lock the eyes.
The left arm extends: dabs: he sits back.   Painting.
   'what seas, what shores?' we ask, as in
   another tongue
he considers the flickering plains of Newington:
    : thought: if I can see him, he can . . .
     hide.   Look again.   Fascination.
What melancholy eyes!   The Greek.

## The Last Voyage of Leif Ericsson, Icelander. *Robin Hamilton*

We knew the time had come when the rats
Leapt overboard and began to swim.   Leif
Called the men together: 'Rotten hulk she is,
Uncaulked bottom, riddled with worms.
Half of us die here.   Only one sound
Dinghy.   Choose.'   And the straws out, and
The drawing.   White faces, or thankful.
Leif drew a long straw for a place.
But some other man, some mother's kinsman
Of his, said: 'Leif, you promised,
Promised your mother, in danger
To shield me.'   So Leif gave his place
For a word spoken in passing.   But
Who that other was who sat beside us
In the boat, no one now knows.

## One Life. *Robin Hamilton*
*For Cesare Pavese, automorito 28 di agosto, 1950*

I. QUESTION

Where do they go, the dead poets—
Not those, bespectacled and laureate, who rest
Contented bones in city churches, but the young
Flicked burning in the mind from ledges,
Or skidding rain-slick wheels across a lorry,
Who stub a cigarete against the rail, and then
Slip backwards off the boat.

What rest for bodies that themselves rejected
Can this earth harbour?   Surely that loam throat
Will cough them out again, refuse digestion
To these sweetmeats, mankind's choicest titbits,
To the young given over to early death.

Keats died in sun-bleached Italy, containing
Just enough breath in faltering lungs
To haul his burden to a foreign ground.

Hart Crane sank into the blue; the sea has finished
Belly, bones, and blood.

After encounters with the night
And stars, now night and stars glow
Through their bones.

Say:
>  Here lies another casualty of our war without
>  Sides or ending; think fairly on his end.
>  He cheated time of a little pain, a little
>  Enjoyment: no more for you will be left at last.

## II. VISION

Perhaps say:
>  Sunlight is an adventure, as is shadow;
>  The edge of the shadow blinds us,
>  But over that boundary, after the first
>  Buckle of perception, sight is clearer.

>  After the shadow, objects pale in the sun,
>  Limpid is insipid in the clear air.
>  In shadow, colours darken and sharpen,
>  Browns grow deeper, greens more like
>  The grass that they are of.

III. EXAMPLE

On little feet, with half-extended claws,
The grey cat walked my chest, placed splayed
Forefeet on each nipple, looked in my eyes
With the weight of years of grey cats walking.

And I asked that anthology of cats, clasped
In one grey pelted body, what a cat must do
When it extends a delicate claw,
Peremptorily taps, as if to say
That it is time to go.
                Cats have the wisdom
Of indifference even to their own pleasures;
Generations of reflective eyes have seen
So much.
        Elemental being does not pale
Within them.   They forget, or remember only
How to forget.
             Generations of cats
Moving in the sun or the shadow, flowing,
A river of claws and eyes, through our mind.

Say:
    This is the lore of cats that man must master,
    That the moment for the moment only matters,
    That each cat holds between its paws
    A fleck of time that to and fro it taps
    Like a trapped mouse.
                Are poems
Man's playing with that moment
While the games of love and death are over?

IV. REASON

But Pavese said:
    She walked the Corso, long legs moving
    From a base of hips, and it came to me,
    So many I had not known who
    Walked like that, so many women
    Delighting in body and mind,
    So many men not talked with,
    Sights unseen, voices unheard,
    Bodies untouched.
                But I had seen enough
    To know, and now all are known,
    All registered and noted down in a clutch
    Of protein chains and muscle movements.
    The time has come to close the book
    By breaking it; more time would be
    Lost time, time to forget.


**White Bread.** *Roderick Hart*


A complete purification, the process
knocks the goodness out of it

till I, the baker, midnight god,
proceed to put a new goodness back.

I cut my sun, my moon and stars
from a loaf of my own.

## Sentence Analysis. *Roderick Hart*

*Sentence*

i

I wondered what had happened to my
coffee and biscuits, and would have gone
to the dining-car had it not been for my
luggage, which might well have been gone
when I got back as no one else was in my
compartment.   Fortunately, it was a non-
smoker, and a gentleman who'd been looking
high and low for one, and had almost gone
the whole length of the train, found my one
relatively empty.   I would have gone then,
but I feared his enterprising eye and
forced myself to wait.   An hour had
gone by before anyone else arrived.
I was about to rise when the agon
ising thought first struck me—my
fellow-travellers, are they accomplices?

ii
In a manner of speaking—they are

iii
The playful scholars kicked their ball
clear over to the dignified side.

All here are agreed that in trying to kick it back
he acted hastily.

It soon had him capering about like an old king
after his crown.

*Analysis*

Some say he was not above referring to himself
in the third person to save what little remained
of his punctilious pedagogy; we'd not pass
this self-imposed severity.


**Tonite.** *Alan Jackson*

tremble, trust not, creep low,
too late!
i am now many,
i walk carrying,
do not bring forth—
what me bastards dragons—
ho no—
i am a quiet lad known
for repose and tempered wrath.
rarely will i go to the theatre
where they play all fancies out,
and pipe my steam en masse.
i have my own most internal
dramatics most theatrical
innards
where nightly to the tune
of ave a neurosis
persons pass and exchange
greedy tot-bites of information,
slander filth and hear hear o-ism.
why part with a dollar to see it done
with frescoes verve and intervals?
   oedipus hamlet all that crowd
of murdering i-ambic ma-lingerers
occupy my brain-pot, that cell, that court,
that judging house, seat and site of the closeted family.

what! most certainly blood doth
not flood me through but printers' ink
and these my talons are only quins.
histories i read merely
to check the facts, corroborate
and set the bounds to my brimming talent
for spectacles and scenes, acts and hacks.

of course kings have burned down cities,
carted off booty, on rafts, through blood,
and good men have been hung, by the teeth, the nails,
                              the hands, the head,
from the crosses of order permanence and greed.
aren't you always at it?   i am.
cops and nazis geysering through
my icy glass of contemplation,
skating and cutting me into ruts,
before the furrowed surface fading
feeds them back to the seethy waters.
every day i ice 'em over, deliberate:
why not?   i'm due three meals a day
like anyone else.   I don't feel called
to sport uniquity yet, though when it stirs
its drug is strong.
                    But those other toiling palaces
of entertainment, archives of secret pacts, called men.
disappoint me terrible.   so rarely they give me
a cry or dance that's from the script i know
they're programmed.   just a bit of sound track sometimes
as you pass, or half an overture when a lad
leans forward: 'I don't know if you ever . . .' and stops—
imagining himself the only one contains
the beast and bastardy that comes along
with the nine proud brain and opposable thumb
of man.   so long in darkness with his own mad kings,

killing mums, sweet maidens et by monsters
and naked formales bending just his way,
he's not seized yet the one embracing fact:
we are the lads the very men
who humped their mums by massy walls
and put our pa's down in an act of congress,
none but us the ghosts and gods, the good and baddies,
who wrought and rended empires the sand still seals . . .
. . . nervously the lad rings off his speech,
smiles sad and says: 'Another time, maybe.   No words
for me to tell what i go through.'

   Brother! sad man, victim, tomb, ark
of all! how could one word of reported truth
fail to dent me, nick and needle exactly
into the furrows and pockets, quarters and grooves
that make my brain yours, yours caesar's and caesar's
the same as that ignorant dull barman feeds us pints.
Audiences, accomplices, witnesses, fellow
fallen, twin birthers, scattered family marked forever
by the contents of our heads, i leave you
to take a bath and comb my hair
in preparation
              for
                TONITE.


**Storm Damage.** *Tom Leonard*

There is a stain on the ceiling above the bed.
Rainwater.   A relic of last year's storm.
It is roughly circular.   Darkest at the centre.
The perimeter is not clearly defined.

Eclipse.   Your body moves on mine.
Your face looks down on me.
The lips are smiling.   The stain
Becomes a halo round your head.

My mind goes back twelve years.
I am a child again, lying in the grass,
Staring into the sky.   Eclipse.

You ask me what I'm thinking.


### The Appetite. *Tom Leonard*

That conversation was a tread,
a trampoline.   'Words are absurd',
it said, and our eyes played
at not being on it, laughing.

We sat facing each other, eating
as if
we sat facing each other, eating.


### Travelling Folk. *Maurice Lindsay*

Cornered in wastes of land, spinnies of old roads
lopped back from the new, where done horses
leaned once on starved haunches, battered cars
nuzzle scrunted bushes and caravans.

Copper-breasted women suckle defiance
at schools inspectors.   Sanitary men
are met with bronze-age scowls.   All to no purpose.
Blown across Europe's centuries, bound only

in piths and withies to settlements not moved
by permanent impermanencies—smoky
violins, dusks gathered from skies
purple as hedge-fruits, or plucked stolen chickens—

these exiles from our human order seed
in the rough, overlooked verges of living,
their stubborn litter filling with vagrancy
the cracks our need of confrontation shows.


**Three Kings Talking.** *Maurice Lindsay*

After it was over, together in the sun,
three specialists in ruling, they compared
  notes, as farmers or carpenters might
warm to each other over the craft they shared.

One said: Although, of course, I'm no
believer in old wives' tales or popular rhymes,
  we have to take new situations
within the accepted context of the times.

For most, the times are never good,
as you both know.  The idea of a saviour
  come as a babe caught people's fancy.
There seemed little chance of riotous behaviour

  over one so young, as long
as I fell in with their much-talked of whim
  that what I had to do was follow
that strange, fast-moving star to come upon him.

The second said: Though it got you here,
we're all of us men of the world, and well aware
    that in the present state of knowledge
one can't account for what makes the simple stare.

    The fact is, in my kingdom there was
unrest, dissatisfaction with the ruling line.
    Nothing you could single out;
rather, a communal waiting for some sign

    that the heat and the flies and the shortage of food
they had to put up with—the sheer injustice of
    their lot—wasn't all that life
had to offer.   I certainly don't mean to scoff

    at this kind of let-out this promised saviour
brings.   If the gold, the frankincense and myrrh
    we've proffered in that stable buys
us relief from unrest, quells any possible stir

    a minority of dissidents might
have fanned up into open revolution,
    our journeys will have been worth while.
A child can't overthrow a constitution.

    The third said: No doubt you're both right.
I don't think I'll forget that mother's face.
    A strange thing, too, the three of us
should come from the earth's ends to this untidy place

    we'd none of us heard of.   Whatever the why
or the wherefore, we've done the sensible thing.
    If the child is holy, he'll be talked of
for longer than any politician or king.

Let us keep silence over the reasons
each of used to get here, and then go
　　our ways, do what needs to be doing,
say what's expected of us, and who's to know

　　of our understandable difficulties?
These three kings parted, each with his own rich train
　　of satisfied diplomacy.
What happened next? They were never heard of again.


## A Break of Patterns. *Maurice Lindsay*

Ranged along the kerb-edge
an almost used-up man, a girl
ready for use, and three or four
whom life has done its best to use.

They wait for a bus. Birds that must hang
tails in space to feel secure,
driven by conservationist nets
from sills of buildings, now stave
themselves on overhead wires;
quavers above an almost used-up
man, a girl ready for use,
and three or four whom life has done.

Legend has it that to receive
a bird's acrid-white dropping
is lucky, holy; a benediction
from Him who breathed upon clay sparrows
when rejects were said to matter.

Myths are no longer popular;
at least not old ones from those times
when more birds blessed fewer people,
equality not yet disproved.

Cheepering, the dark hysteria
settles, and benedictions plop
upon an almost used-up man,
a girl ready for use, and three
or four whom life has done its best to.

They toss indignant glances at
the Corporation Cleansing Department,
the Minister of Transport and
the Minister of Communications.
The anger falls down like droppings,
since no one can communicate
to no one just what may have been
—or how—disturbed by buildings, bus-stops,
or people, queues of people, queues of . . .

**Subjective projective.** *Maurice Lindsay*

amber
slow up
red red—

clicky clack clack domenico scarlatti
open the window
breathe fresh pollution
quite a belly that girl's carrying
wonder if she got it in bed
or in the back of some man's car
defending womens' right to freedom
whatever the christ that is—

did he spit down that drain
just because the drain was there
gaping up at him
god
the permissive society —

hairy enough to be a poet
too damn many of them
any bugger can be a poet
now that you can't nail thoughts with rhyme
or even have thoughts
too old fashioned for collapsing society
the sunday critics cry
wishing they could write poems themselves
probably why they cry —

girls get pregnant
men spit down drains
poems arent so very different —

red domenico
ruffled cock in spanish courtyard
who the hell cares anyway —

art for arts sake
drains for drains sake
girls for producing girls for producing girls for —

green green
go go go
i accelerate you accelerate they accelerate
we move forward

**Revelation.** *Elizabeth Lochhead*

I remember once being shown the black bull
When a child at the farm for eggs and milk.
They called him Bob—as though perhaps
You could reduce a monster
With the charm of a friendly name.
At the threshold of his outhouse, someone
Held my hand and let me peer inside.
At first, only black
And the hot reek of him.   Then he was immense,
His edges merging with the darkness, just
A big bulk and a roar to be really scared of,
A trampling, and a clanking tense with the chain's jerk.
His eyes swivelled in the geat wedge of his tossed head.
He roared his rage.   His nostrils gaped like wounds.
And in the yard outside
Oblivious hens picked their way about.
The faint and rather festive tinkling
Behind the mellow stone and hasp was all they knew
Of that Black Mass, straining at his chains.
I had always half-known he existed—
This antidote and Anti-Christ, his anarchy
Threatening the eggs, well rounded, self-contained—
And the placidity of milk.

I ran, my pigtails thumping alien on my back in fear,
Past the big boys in the farm lane
Who pulled the wings from butterflies and blew up frogs with straws.
Past thorned hedge and harried nest,
Scared of the eggs shattering—
Only my small and shaking hand on the jug's rim
In case the milk should spill.

**The Gentle Ambush.** *George Macadam*

No fabulous warrior came hunting
For your life.   Whatever scythed you
Down wore no emblematic garb
Nor magically spirited you away
Through solid wall, stone wood or glass,
And left a rough replica
When your flesh and blood alive
Became an effigy of clay.
Nothing came: all was in the leaving.
And no ghost haunts the rooms
Your presence filled.   What quickens
A half recognition on the stairs
That creak, in the suit holding yet
Your shape, or in the roses
That you hadn't time to prune—
The gentle ambush I'm helpless to resist—
Is: no one's there.   And absence
Stares me blankly in the face.


**Near Hamsterley.** *George MacBeth*

       At the edge of the road,
as I drove near pines, there were drifts
of snow still.
          I stopped, and walked
in the bare wood.
            As I climbed down
over scattered needles, light fell
slanting through branches.
              I paused, and squatted
by the long slide of scooped white
along the ride.

A spider crawled
on the stripped hide of my coat,
and I brushed it off.
                    As I climbed,
working again towards the car,
something stopped me.
                         It lay on its side
by a rough wall, close to the road,
with its back to a stump.
                         Against the wood
its bloat udder looked inflamed.
                                   Its fleece
was the colour of dirty snow
in the dead stillness.
                    No birds creaked
or twigs broke.
                 Its legs were rigid,
stuck out awkwardly, like a child's
toy over-turned.
                 It must have tried
to kneel, make a ball
to hold the cold out, the heat in,
hunched by the wall.
                    It must have waited
with all its patience for night to end
and the sun rise.
                  I saw it now,
standing above it in my fleece coat
like a false shepherd.
                       And so, turning,
I walked back to the car
and drove on.
              As the wheels grazed
those heaped falls of driven fleece
from the sky, I wondered why
that one sheep had died.

All round,
on the moor, a hundred stood
and cropped a spare grass.
                    In the light
sluicing their soft backs, as one
they moved and survived.
                    I stopped the car
again by a damp verge,
and got down to look.
                    It was Saturday,
between the death and the resurrection,

Already, the first lambs were out.

### The Being Highly Intelligent. *Brian McCabe*

Being highly intelligent
I may choose to invent the wheel this morning.
I may then decide
Intelligently
Either to leave the wheel alone
Or to use the wheel.
Of course
I may put the wheel to most
Intelligent use
and
I may
Misuse the wheel.

Being highly intelligent
I may never love the wheel.
Love
Does not
Make the wheel
Go round.
But being highly intelligent
I may also never hate the wheel.

Only its footprints in my dawn.

## Inward Bound. *Norman MacCaig*

On the Calton Hill
the thirteen pillars
of this failed Parthenon
    made more Greek by the cargo boat
    sailing between them
    on the cobwebby water of the Firth
should marry nicely with the Observatory
in the way complements
    each observing the heavens
    in its different way
except that in this case half a pomegranate
is clapped against half
a workmanlike potato.
These pillars fit better
with the man sat scrunched between them.
    Journeys level differences and who are
    more hospitable
    than nomads?
Even his raincoat might have warded off the weather
all the way from Thebes.   The scrip by his side
is filled with Scotch olives.

The illumination of new problems
burns on the tiderace that headlongs
    straight as Princes Street
from dawn to dusk—as the sideslipping sun
makes flares of the windows in the North British Hotel.
    They'll die back through ashes into windows
    and prove, tomorrow, illuminations
    are not answers.

And the man between the pillars
will be replaced by another

making through the windows of the world
towards his Ithaca and proving
there's no end to the windings
or the journeyings.

The Castle pretends No
as though, having choked the flume of a volcano,
it could make history gag
by sticking in its throat
   forgetting that once
   round its harsh crag wheeled
   spent crossbow arrows
   that splashed in the Nor' Loch whose water
   translated them to ducks.

Swans still go over, seaplaning down
to Dunsappie, and geese
squeezing the bulbs of old fashioned motor horns
waver high over the Queen's Bath House
their flat bills
pointing straight to Benbecula —
   unknotted thread of journeying
   one of a web too tangled
   to have a centre.
Journeys.   Mine were
as wide as the world is
from Puddocky to Stockaree
   minnows flash in a jar
   splinters of light
   in the bright water
   and a ten-inch yacht
   in the roaring forties of Inverleith Pond
   crumples like a handkerchief
till the web enlarged

choked once with a zeppelin
that dropped the beginning of the end of the world
on the Grassmarket
to enclose places that grew two selves
their own and the one I made of it
and people that became two multitudes
their own and the one I invented
and ideas
whose war of attrition still goes on
in my only skull—how many casualties
are marked with no cross
in the Dark backward.

Dark as the stairs and closes of the Canongate
and the West Bow. They smell of piss
that used to smell of piss and pomanders
and are gothic and gloomy enough
for a weak mind
to hallucinate the shadows
with shades—
with the perukes and cloaks
of foppish and lousy gangsters—
the costume jewellery
in poor bedraggled Scotland's diadem.

No journey is ever ended
Greyfriars and the melancholy double-blanks
in Warriston Kirk Yard
are answers to that
or reversible.
And most haunting of all
are the ones that were never made.
Out of my speech—Toll Cross dialect of Anglo-Scots—
I trespassed over the border
into Gaelic and glimpsed

facts and the decoration of facts
that now only glimmer in my mind
like a coin at the bottom of a well.

Such a long way back
such a long way in
   when the famous killers were in Chicago
   and Glasgow was a mean City
   and Welsh miners sang in London Streets
   and Scotch potatoes were lifted by Irish girls
when the world to me
was Heaven in its infancy all rosy and
spangled with islands whose villages
sent out drifters, lug sails
   they tethered themselves to a mile of nets
   between the Shiants and the
   mainland of Harris and waited nightlong
   for the herring that didn't come.
I fishing for cuddies off Craig Lexie
going for a few sheep
to an island off an island off an island
was a millionaire of sunlight and summer winds
freeman of a kingdom behind a kingdom
far traveller among spinningwheels
explorer
and without knowing it a miser
stuffing the bag of my mind
with sovereigns
I've been spending ever since.
   What water ever flashed
      ever flashes
   like the water in the Red Well
      in lecture rooms suburban buses
   and what mysteries of distance
   and unguessable arrivals

were not crammed in the hold of the *Eilean Glas*
anchored in Scalpay Bay
and stramed by the tide in a due line
pointing to the Clisham.

(The fishergirls sang on the pier.
Their songs had nothing to do
with the blood and the guts of herring.

Though one had no thought for me
to this day when I think of her
I feel new wounds

remembering
that flashing knife,
those bandaged fingers.)

Such a journey back
such a journey in—
it expands it brings closer
places and non-places
   as though to journey
   in a stone—
through dreams and their extensions—
across the border of the farthest idea.
These things come down into
the region of the possible—I feel
I could fly without feathers
   —and no talk of Icarus.

Every step
is a moonlanding, my feet sink
in unpredictables and astonishments.
They carry me to where
I look down on the brawny continents
and the slipshod oceans fixed by distance
into stillness.

Darkness I love darkness I am motored
by darkness
   the soil flows smoothly over
   my two-way fur, I paddle it
   aside
which has its own dusky galaxies
the glimmerings of darkness in darkness
on which someone
will make a glimmer-landing
and send messages up
as new flowers.
   A shape disturbs some fibres
   inside my head with bracts
   and foetal stamens and a tinted vapour
   of possible flowers smelling
   of a time to come, of a distance
   not yet thought of.

Two apples plus two oranges equals
four (fruit) abstractions.   The dimension
where they equal four concretes
particular and abstract in one
calls for its explorers and will be
explored.
   Imagine an imagination that is wholly
   the man it is the imagination of
   how he/it will with the little lift
   of a revelation carry the imaginable
   into the possible and the possible
   into the actual—new fleets
   making their landfall simultaneously
   in the five ports of knowledge
   and hoisting ashore their
   unimaginable cargoes.

Can't you hear the voices
   the snarling the condescending the terrified
   the envious squeak the robust hello boy bellow
saying such a place would be
thinking without thinking
living without living
dying without dying—
forgetting that they know no more than anyone else
of the understanding of understanding.
   That leaf—
   on the branch
   in the pool
   in my mind—
   signed itself in triplicate
   and of the three statements it made
   I could read only the third
   and it the most corrupt.
I can't make myths I can't make fables.
When I try to invent one
a true crow swallows real cheese
and a real fox
doesn't like grapes anyway.

Yet I am peeked at by possibilities that vanish
when I turn to stare at them as though a fable
were signalling desperately from the future to
now.
   Possibilities! said the man to me
   by the Blackford Pond.—They put in one hand
   the rose of all the world and
   in the other a parcel with a tick in it.
   I agreed, gravely, and watched, gravely, a swan
   floating like a lotus
   with a white snake in it.

And no talk of Icarus.
—Yet for every Icarus
there was a Daedalus.
And for each who remembers
the pitching, the alighting of that maniac man-bird
how many remember
the curled cloud
the ship sailing by
and the white, sudden

tombstone of water.

Now by the Nelson Monument          and an eye
   such a congruence—an arm and an eye
   as Freudian as the phallic symbol
   he's erected on
I die another of the innumerable deaths
life can be made to seem to consist of
   the easiest ones, the ones with resurrections
and cheerfully thankfully bequeath to myself
journeys remembered
to be amicable divided between
my romantic my classical
my Gothic my Georgian
my orchestral plainsong
me.

**Pruning.** *David McDuff*

All evening long I have watched
the dog running slowly after
the man who cuts the arms
and legs from his trees
that hang in the air quite helplessly.

All evening I have watched
the slow climb that will bring
at its end a nest of fear
thatched with feathers and dead
insects, a cluster breaking the mind,
hindering sleep and wakefulness.
Since it will be cold in the gardens
I will fill your eyes now with all the sun's eyes,
since there will be no more bread
I will breathe in your nostril the seed of all the cornfields,
since there will be no place to be
I will build
in the seconds that it takes our shadows to touch
a cell of thread
from which to watch
the moon take the colours away, the single steps
go pruning over the hill.


**Casa Maremmana.** *David McDuff*

In that house the minutes are growing
too scarce, and between them the space
long and difficult.   In that gleam,
in that night all movement slows to a trail,
subsides.   The doors in that house
are opened alone by the left hand.
Turn the key away from you as you see
as you ought to but dare not;
turn the key in the door and see
the plain turned to glass, over dead
convolvulus the spider's thread
which breaks at the touch of sight.

## Then One Morn. *Tom McGrath*

*For John Tripp*

Then one morn the president awakes
to find his lazybird gone,
the telephone dead, he is alone
in the big decision building—
and the war must go on,

the president walks down into the streets
(still in pyjamas) where he meets
no-one, every door is open, empty cars—
and the war? he is asleep,

he must be. Help, the presidential eye
is dazzled by an angel, white wings,
wide as in his childhood books,
the sun is oblivious in the sky—

and the war is over
and the war is dead,
there are two kinds of angels,
There is only one world.


## Heroes. *Tom McGrath*

Three men make a circle
their slender swords drawn,
plumes in their hats,
moustaches atwirl,

ha got us a girl each
several goblets of wine,
today in the sunshine
we feel mighty fine,

for we are the cavaliers
we will swing on chandeliers
make miraculous escapes
interrupt several rapes

and they will write novels
make films of our feats
and no-one will say how we stank
and had syphilis—
in our laughing eyes and apple cheeks
they will catch the arrogance
of the present

aha my athos aha my pathos
douglas fairbanks and tyrone power
D'Artagnan D'Artagnan


**Poems for 'Poets'.** *Tom McGrath*

1. 'it smites us into darkness . . .

   and so we pop up,
   a quarrelsome paranoiac mess
   of talking men,
   (and there's some women too,
   talking and talking
   in this bleak land of ours
   that all of us are loath to call
   our home

   talking and arguing
   and puking—passing out
   in pubs, on wonder drugs

and flying with the best of them,
the wildest of them,
raging through the maddest nights

only to land back down in Scotland,
for God's sake, secondrate Scotland,
Scotland with no language,
Scotland always looking back
—never quite remembering—
Scotland always on the point of
never quite arriving:

we are the Scottish writers.
we are bound to be crazy.
history has always happened,
somewhere else.

and so we pop up
talking and puking,
trying to believe
that we can do it too,
that if we say it
there's still someone there
to listen,
there's still some point
to be talking it to.
> (for Tom Buchan and all Scotch
> writers, afraid and lonely men
> who never learned to talk—
> I know why you're going
> to Amsterdam.

2. Personal Statement.

The function of art
is the corruption of
the human spirit.

I will make your children
drug addicts and perverts.
I will disease their flesh
and fracture their minds,
irreparably.

I will create Oedipus, Hamlet and Baudelaire.
I will create academies to instil them
into innocent minds.

Your fresh-cheeked son
will be your own lamenting ghost.

I will give them comfort.
I will give them culture.
I will give them celluloid to look at
and plastic to listen to,
the history of art
in paperback.

I will create a spiritual wilderness
that will seem to them full of meaning.
They will aspire to the mythical
and my curse will take effect.
They will search for the heroic
and grow sick at trivia.
Confused and hesitant, they will regard
a thousand aesthetic monuments,
unable to decide.

And while they wonder,
the animals will take their daughters.

I will call them bourgeois
and they will feel guilty.
I will blast out image at them
of the wars their comfort feeds upon,
the wars they are responsible for
and we can do nothing about.

They will put pennies in cans
and march in protest.
They will take strange drugs
and lose themselves in dreams.
They will waken in hospitals
in anonymous white gowns.
They will forge words
to bless their degradation.

They will grow old
and fester.

They will become the ghosts of their fathers.
The world will call them scholars
and they will enter libraries.
never to be seen again.

Their flesh will become parchment.
And I will drain away their soul.

The function of art
is the corruption of
the human spirit.

## Pabay. *Stewart McIntosh*

Candle-lit farmhouse shadows
marching off into the dark
sea whimpering through the wind
or wavelets wheedling round
rocks sipping nettle beer splashing
as Margie sings in her bath
writing words which tip-toe away
from me into the gloom where
surrounded by enamels and tiny
pots Stuart paints his rainbow
rings on a tiny island by an
island by an island by a
continent which isn't in our sphere

Dawn
bending over backwards to repair
the boat our tenuous link with
civilisation waiting for the tide
to float or sink it with
expectant eyes surprised to see
visitors on our beach come by
boat for a pic-nic with quiet
distaste for the way we're living
they buy some pendants, dangling small
talk groping for a wavelength too
weak and tiny for them to receive
in these wireless mountains
He paints all day I jig
saw with my words butter
flies and rabbits dancing in
my mind long discussions mass
turbating the worth of our work

ing in the kitchen Margie
can fulfil what words and
pictures never will. . . .
prematurely leaving our chrysalis
with wings damp and
limp round the city hawking
rings and pendants while the
doves are starving on Pabay.


**Diane.** *Stewart McIntosh*

Tired and dejected hair dripping
wet trying to hitch a ride
up Loch Lomondside.   Her mini
stops short, a shaking wheezing
white terror.   I stare in surprise
surprise I've waited nearly four
hours for this moment.   'Cumonn.
Gerrin.' she drawls we jerk
off and smash puddles northwards.

'Road's crawling with bloody
hitchers' she complains, 'but
I liked the tired way you
smiled.'   We talk, she teaches
poetry in Australia, I read
her some of mine, she's impressed.
Wow!   The gorgeous doll's impressed!

Tired now but laughing still
we tumble over to Skye
I fall asleep and talk
all night she listens
and cackles evilly into

her cornflakes tantalising
me with what I might
or might not have said.

Then out on the road to laugh
uproariously round the island
the car barking and yelping
with glee cocking its leg
at passing places nipping the
heels of lumbering buses.   Screech
of brakes and out she leaps
sprinting up the drunken
road sandals flapping bangles
clinking mad hoops flying
round her pants.   'You crazy
kite you can't catch sheep!
It's not allowed!'   Chokes back
into the driving seat 'I only
wanted to FEEL him!'

Zoom back to the caravan
fling her psychedelic suitcase
into the panting car.   Swop
'phone numbers—world apart
yet closer than that.   At last
whoop of laughter as she unleashes
the mini and they chase bumble
bees to the ferry together.   Some
times I wish I'd kissed her.

## At Kilbryde Castle. *Lorn M. Macintyre*

Through the white winter palace
of the royal forest
our horses pace on muffled hooves,
past tree-stumps upholstered with snow
like the toppled foot-stools of courtesans
who have fled the revolution,
leaving the sable stole
trailing over the rhododendrons'
ramshackle sofa.

Jilted hinds stare
into the cracked mirrors of pools
and eyes like forgotten cigarettes
in white saucers glare
as I unsheath my shotgun,
snap in two cartridges.

My love, you reel
in the saddle
as the black tracer
of the woodcock
bursts from the shrubbery,
and the cold war ends.

**Ruin.** *Lorn M. Macintyre*

At last I have found an image
for your ruin.
I have translated
Gaelic proverbs
and the sayings of seers
with their blue stones
and black fears
for the future.
This image will not be found
in razed crofts
or rusted swords buried
in time's rotten thatch:
it will not be found
in the anxious lady
consulting the watch
when Culloden is long over.

This image is in the salmon cobble
with the shattered spine
beached beyond the water-line
in the time
of the record run.

Blood has stained
the gunnels
on which countless salmon,
clean, slippery
as pure thoughts
were brained.

## Clean Salmon. *Lorn M. Macintyre*

I posed and at twenty paces
south of the toppled wishing-stone
in the peace after the storm
flicked the glamorous salmon fly
on the white silk handkerchief
you had spread on the lawn
by the despondent daffodils,
With a duelling pistol
looted from father's library
I shot the rusty fin
breaking surface
on the waterlogged sundial.
In the stormy dawn
I sailed a leaking skiff
without compass, without chart
through the notorious reefs,
brought you back plankton.

You are still unimpressed.
You sit in the bay window,
in the blinding light of my memory,
bent over intricate embroidery.
This day is ordinary,
except for the ripple
of salmon in the estuary,
and no nets ready.

## In Memory of Angus John Campbell. *Lorn M. Macintyre*
*20th Hereditary Captain of Dunstaffnage Knight of Malta*

> And I am in despair that time may bring
> Approved patterns of women or of men
> But not that selfsame excellence again
> YEATS *The Municipal Gallery Revisited*

Turning and turning
your small coins
over and over
in superstitious awe
under a new moon
on your ruined avenue

you saw
that bulldozers
would blaze
a new road
through your policies
to the accursed south,
and the setter's soft mouth
tighten round
the warm grouse.

Feeble seas
deposit their pollution
on your once-private shore
where Sassenach tourists
smile behind cheap sun-glasses
and the southern whore
poses for the Instamatic.
Sassenach wrists

flick the mass-produced fly
over your once-private burn.

Yet you resisted the clapboard slum
accumulating under the walls
of your ruined keep
where you would sleep
on Midsummer's night,
unafraid of the restless dead.

There is no solution.
The frantic wings
of the scuttled grouse
are clocks
that cannot retreat.
Dynamite has erased
the ruin of your house

and there is blood
on the ancestral sheet
while we, crazed
by commonness,
call down the patient hawks.


**The Cosmonaut; Hero-Three.** *Alastair Mackie*

The hero noo is twa or three.
'Whaur twa or three are gaithered in thy name'
the hero is the haill o them.
This is technology.

The yirth's frieze o the famous
auld-farrant captains, deid
wi a hantle o honours on their heid,
like Spartan Leonidas

say or John Graham nearer hame,
that sang's ower and done.
In this melee we hae won
for hero a collective name.

There's nae room here for the classic
cavalry chairges, rear-gaird ploys—
action, the undevallin noise
o the individualistic.

Mair mechanisms nor men,
we fit aneither perfect;
we are thirled like the elect
tae predestination.

Leevin forekent, sleepin forekent,
aye and deein gin it were tae be.
In a wey we're like the trinity
three persons, ae instrument.

Aince Odysseus in his seggy-boat
guddled aboot i the aidle-pool
o Europe. Ae Homer's singin broo'll
no be makar o't—

oor Odyssey. It waits its heroes.
(We staun yet on the door-sill. The apen-furth
o the solar system's like a hearth
for haill flotillas o's

tae hame for) But no jist yet.
Heroes need time tae mak.
We've tint oor wee egos. Ahint oor back
they've drapped like a rocket.

## Lines for Mallarmé. *Alastair Mackie*

Aye, white is fearfu and the speerit's sweer.
The birds threep threep.   I maun thole aince mair
the nakit arctic o the page.   White sheets
are waggin till the lift their fare-ye-weel.
O tae prie distance and the sea's mirk wines.
Ower the horizon the airn eerands gang.
I list the dappled leids the day-daw prents
o the lift's uncoonted blads.   The book o days.
And the nichts showdin i the gaup o starns.
Faces I niver saa nor fremmit ports
trysts wi the horizon I niver kept.
The hamecomin o the een.   The herbour
hugs.   I staun and ee the coasters, back and
fore and you, your hands amang the white claes.
Eident the airn ower the airnin boord.
Hoo sma that sea is in the gloamin licht!


## Mongol Quine. *Alastair Mackie*

Elbucks on the herbour wa
the mongol quine
collogues
wi hersel.

Her blond ba-heid wags
frae side to side.
Noo she's a clock-hand
noo a croon.

Wha said grace and grouwin
tae this mistak?
A ban was on her
frae furder back.

Nievie nievie nack nack
whit hand 'll ye tak tak?
She got the wrang hand
and didna pan oot.

She got pig's een
a bannock face
and hurdies that rowed
like twa muckle bools.

She wints for naething.   Yet
she's singin till the distance.
Ayont the hert-brak her een
are set for ever on an unkent airt.


## Châteaux en Ecosse. *Alastair Mackie*

'Lauchin at the puffin-lowe'.
I mind her yet hurklin ower the ingle
the deid auld body o my grandmither
croonin tae the firelicht unkent wirds.
'Puffin-lowe'.   The winter gleed lauchit back
at her Lallans.

'Fit sa ye there?'
The poker duntit on the coals in time.
I maun hae dwaumed at her speirin yon
and drooned in the hert's bluid o the aizles.
I didna ken the jingle was an orphelin
that had langsyne tint the family o the tongue
and quavered noo i the auld wife's craig.
It nott a bleeze like yon tae gar it spik.

'Aa the widden-dremers'.
Whit did she mean? it was her deid forebears
(and mine) makkin ballants frae a bleeze
on winter nichts, workin fowk brakkin oot
o history and their crubbit lives, gaupin
at a lowe. And forby it was mebbe me.
Then and noo.

'Biggin castles i the air.'
Frae hyne awa I hear an auld wife sing
a kinna dregy till an ingle-gleed.
Here's me blawin on the cauld ess o her tongue
tae bigg, châteaux en Ecosse, thae bit poems.


**Scots Pegasus.** *Alastair Mackie*

Oor Scots Pegasus
is a timmer naig
wi a humphy back and cockle een.

He ettles tae flee
but his intimmers are fu o the deid chack.
Gin he rins ava
he pechs sair.
And spales drap aff like sharn.

He's fed on bruck
scranned frae aa the airts
This gies him the belly thraw
and yon etten and spewed look.

Makars whiles
fling a leg ower his rig-bane
and crank the hunnle on his spauld.

He taks a turn roon the park
but niver gets aff the grun
or oot o the bit.
This mishanter's caad
in some stables—
a new voice in Lallans.

Ithers, brither Scots
gie him the hee-haw.

The hert o the nut is this—
naebody, dammt, kens the horseman's wird.


**Our Bull.** *Alasdair Maclean*

He has the hips and shoulders
of an exaggerated Mr Universe.
Viewed from the front
he's the width of a whole field.

His kingdom is red-rimmed.
Everything that moves in it he stops.
Everything that's stopped he moves.

Pressure builds up in him periodically.
His sides heave and quiver.
Jets of steam gush from his nostrils.
One more pound per square inch
and he'd explode.

Even at rest in the long grass
he's still a metaphor for danger:
the round black hump of his back,
horn tips rising over it,
bobs menacingly in the green swell.

Standing he dominates the landscape.
Tourists sweat their way past him
at fifty yards or more,
feeling with outstretched toes
for the next foothold.
The women say nothing;
a tendency to dawdle when almost safe
reveals the difference
between the fear they'd own to
and the one they hide.

No blame to them.
He moves from legend to reality
with ease, and brings
the best part of his story with him.
His bellowing's preliminary only.   He delivers.

Yet he will follow a cow
about to come in heat
so modestly he seems to shrink.
He accepts her insults meekly
and keeps his weapon sheathed.
One thrust through the vitals pays for all.

Or in a randy mood, no cows available,
he'll stab the air, semen dripping from him

in the ambiguous prodigality of nature.
Our bull is state-owned
and will be salvaged by and by.
Someone in an office somewhere
charts his progress.
Calf production is plotted against time
and the curve goes down.

I was given once
the chance to watch a bull,
his service done,
being poleaxed in a slaughterhouse.
He died so quickly and so heavily
I trembled.   Before my heart
had ceased to register the shock
he was chained and swung,
a bucket hung from his horns
and his throat tapped.

**Bathrooms.** *Alasdair Maclean*

They are terrifying places.
They are white and sterile and glittering.
Nine tenths of them is below the surface.

They squat at the centre of all your houses.
All your twists and turns end in this one room.

They are where you may safely be yourself.
Nothing you do moves them or shocks them.

They are where you cleanse yourself for courtship
and where when it is over you wash your love away.

They are where you note the inner processes:
the piping hidden by the bland facade
and the jump nestling beneath the skin.

They are where the windows are frosted
to stop you from looking out
and where the doors have locks
so that no one can get in to join you.

They are where one day your vision clears for good.
You can see through the man in the mirror.
You can see the sadness depositing inside his heart.
You can see the shelf in his mind where the razor is kept.


**Last.** *Gerald Mangan*

> *Off he gat;*
> *And cheerful was he. At the stern he sat,*
> *And steered right artfully . . .*
> CHAPMAN'S *Homer*

There is not a face now that, being
Among the last, does not for me contain every brick of that
City in the mere line of its eye; that won't
Disarm what was intractable, or blurt out
Whatever the landscape would never have
Confided.
        And even that wave of the harbour-
Master's hand (the last rock to diminish before an
Ocean) sinks under this gaze of mine he can't see.   The leaden
Motion of an event foregone—woven, before the
Act, into some text of its own history.   I had never these
Eyes, before launching out where the
Rest only cast their lines.


**Double Bed.** *Gerald Mangan*

A sky is dove-tailed into chimney-
pots.   From just a black possibility, it
thinks up a blue and blocks it
with white.   Dissatisfied, another blue.   Back
from the toilet, your palms smell of
carbolic.   Head first, a sun pops out.

Abstracted, the mirror watches the wall
behind the bed—follows Sunday some
paces behind.   I search it for sun, the damp-
stains on the ceiling for faces.   It
searches me for mirrors.   You'll have to

take your coffee black.   Downstairs, the
pendulum clock blooms nine; I play a blues
record soft, the kettle shakes and the
sun wades in at last.   Drinking, I search
your face for mine.   You
search my face for yours.


**Motorway.** *Gerald Mangan*

Seventy miles north between four and
Five a.m.   Each single move is a dead
Virgin—as pure and as safe; a straight ruled
Over graph-paper without a waver.   A camera
Would find no difficulties, would blur nothing
Between frames—the verge one oblong green, even the
Accesses fashioned after sheer forward movement.   There

Is no such thing as a single blade of grass.   At
Point A or B only the eye can rest and two consecutive
Rains fall; between these are long curves which
The soles of feet do not even feel.

## At St Andrew's, Golspie. *John Manson*

I tread on rows of thick flat red slabs,
Turning over the hay with my foot.
Many are plain; some might have been scratched by a nail.
Initials, names, dates—
This Beureal Pleas belongs to John Sothrland, 1731.
A half-drawn margin without legend.
A border inscribed on the level part of a field.

Cruciform kirk, tide-marked harling,
Bare surrounds of windows, gables, eaves, doors.
I press down the tongue of the sneck.
The stalls have been scrubbed with light grey paint.

The Sutherland loft cost Fourty one pd. odds, 1739.
Initials, Arms, Sans Peur; worm-drilled varnish.
I climb the outside stair, not for the ordinary,
Rusting footscraper on either side.    Locked.

Who sat in it?    A Roman senator
On a red plinth on Beinn a' Bhraghaidh?
The historian says 'The transformation in agriculture . . .'
Was 'not without a corresponding period
Of social tension and upheaval'!    What social tension was that?


## The Way the Wind Blows. *A. S. Martin*

Each tree uprooted by the gale, a monument;
the people seeming to stop still, watching,
like unknown sheiks wrapping themselves against
a showering desert, entranced in darkness.

Then she comes walking, her hair alive in the air
walking as if stopped still, leaning, head touching
sharp-edged leaves which swarm
like locusts homing on some destruction.

The lights of the new school grasp her as the gates
shut.   I follow, frightened, with the books which teach me
knowledge in my hands, learning the power of her scent
and which way the wind blows.


**The Polonius Version.** *Irene May*

'Sane let us grant him.   Even in his
Maddest moments.   Did I then choose wrongly?

The absent heir, favourite of the people,
Was just a student in Wittenberg.
An erratic youth—even then.

True, he is handsome and talented,
And well versed in court manners,
The usual accomplishments—duelling,
Writing billets doux and speaking blank verse—
But not a king.   He knows it as well as I.
Whereas his uncle, though a grosser man
Than his late Majesty, is mature, experienced,
And (I admit) very persuasive . . .

In short, the man on the spot
Got the job.   And together we swung Council
Our way.   A brief note was sent to Hamlet,
Informing him of our decision,
Together with an invitation to the Wedding.

I trust I have acted in the best interests of the State.'

### Cape Cornwall. *Paul Mills*

Walls, wires, fields, and a crumbly road
Show up beyond me the misty space,
While a warning drones through the fog.
A big insect.   A deep chord
On the keyboard of the sea, untraceably slow
Music in a vast room.

Some without footholds, long floors of rock
Tilt into foam or cloud.   To a gull
Or a bat, this edge is not their world's.
I must be a lizard to survive,
Entering its alert stealth and ease,
Growing comfortable with this atmosphere,
Body homing round jut and crack, carefully,

And now tensed, balanced, gripping, holding
My weight down to the centre of ledge then ledge
Which it takes one step to remove—
Just shifting my treacherous strength
To make a fulcrum of nothing—

How big is the inch my foot reaches
Down towards and finding, clenches?
What surprised yell must I not hear
To stay on, or how far not turn my head
To be bumped over full in the face
By the crystal breakage of crushed stone teeth
Somewhere to which side of me?

A red admiral blown out helplessly
Into the Atlantic that eats England
That ends here, shows how much easier it is
To be that careless stumbling wave failing wave,
That I could reach by stepping into air,

To become nothing,
Like that wave that falls back into the sea,
No longer in danger of becoming anything.


### Thunder. *Paul Mills*

Across the garden, empty deck chairs
Arranged in friendly groups
Knees touching, exchanging whispers.
The wind strengthens in their sails,
Flapping them nowhere, irritably,

And the guests have all gone indoors
In case of thunder, huddling close
Like mirrors admiring each other.
Outside, rain gust and light
Flash across the grass.

We must cover up all shining objects.
The storm will break them.   See
In the lightning the glasshouse
Whitens suddenly, unable to move,
Its glass world exposed and terrified.

In the city, people with glass skulls
Are struggling home.   Walls, clothes
Of glass.   Glass bodies, paling
Of colour as the sky darkens.
In doorways, those that are sheltering

Are doing glass things, delicate hands
Polishing their reflected shelves,
Then, growing silent and anxious.
I look at my hands, they have
Already grown shiny, shaped with age.

And as the raged sky strikes out
I see nothing to shelter me,
And nothing to shelter, reflecting all.
And my own brittle body, careful on the earth.
Which is still the earth, green and still, appeased.


**Aunt Zoë.** *William Montgomerie*

Long ago
long before you were born
Uncle John brought his bride home
from England
a foreign country to the south
where father had never been

In the front Room
she leans slightly on
her elegant long umbrella
mother's is black and useful
with a curved handle

I stare out of my shyness at
her hat
cartwheels rattle on granite down Dalmarnock Street
mother's hatpins have black beads
not butterflies
and she pulls her hat
on

Under her veil
my new aunt kisses mother
shakes hands with my father and
from a silver box
gives me a speck of menthol

that burns my tongue
She never sits down
stands there
leaning slightly
the last flounce of her skirt
on our faded carpet

From the height of
her tiny waist
I am still staring at
the toe of her red shoe

## Stobhill. *Edwin Morgan*

*The Doctor*

Yes, I agreed to perform the abortion.
The girl was under unusual strain.
I formed the opinion that for personal reasons
and home circumstances her health would suffer
if pregnancy was not terminated.
She was unmarried and the father was unknown.
She had important exams to sit,
her career would be jeopardized, and in any case
she went in mortal fear of her father
(who is himself, as it happens, a doctor)
and believed he would throw her out the house
if her preganancy was discovered.
Accordingly I delivered her seven months' baby
without complications.   It was limp and motionless.
I was satisfied there was no life in it.
Normal practice was followed: it was placed
in a paper disposal bag and sent
to the incinerator.   Later to my surprise
I was told it was alive.   It was then returned
and I massaged its chest and kept it warm.
It moved and breathed about eight hours.
Could it have lived?   I hardly think so.
You call it a disturbing case?   Disturbing
is a more emotive word that I would choose
but I take the point.   However, the child
as far as I was concerned was dead
on delivery, and my disposal instructions
were straight and without melodrama.
There is, as sheriff and jury will agree,
an irony for students of the human condition

(and in this case who is not?)
in the fact that the baby was resuscitated
by the jogging of the bag on its way to the incinerator.
I hope that everything I have said is clear.

## The Boilerman

Ay well, the porter brought this bag doon
(he'd come fae the operatin theatre like)
an he sayed it wis fur burnin.
Ah tellt him it would have tae wait,
ah had tae clean the fire oot first,
say hauf an oor, then it could go in.
So he goes away an leaves the bag,
it wis on a big pile of bags, like, all ready
fur tae go in.   Anyway, ah gote the fire up,
ah starts throwin bags in the incinerator,
an ah'm luftin this wee bag an
ah hear a sorta whimperin—cryin like—
an ah can feel somethin breathin
through the paper.   Whit did ah dae?
Ah pit it on a binch, near the hote pipes.
An ah goes up thae sterrs for the porter.
Asks him, What wis in that bag?
He says, A foetus.   Ah says, What's that?
A kiddy, he says.   D'ye ken it's alive? ah says.
He says, Yes.   Ah says, It's a bluidy shame,
is it no?   He says, Ay it's a bluidy shame.
But the sleekit bugger never let dab
when he brought the bag.   All he sayed wis burn it
an that's the God's truth.   It's bad enough
whit the doctors dae, but he'd have been a murderer
if ah hadny heard the wean cryin—
Christ, it wis hinging ower the fire—
may-be a quick death in thae degrees,

but ahcouldny sleep for nights,
thinkin aboot it, couldny sleep
an och, ah still think what's the use,
ah didny save the kiddy's life.
It canny have been meant tae live.
An yet ye'd wonder, wid ye no?

## The Mother

I've no idea who the father is.
I took a summer job in a hotel
in the Highlands, there was a party, I
got drunk, it must have happened then
but I remember nothing.   When I knew
I was pregnant I was almost crazy,
it seemed the end of everything.
My father—it was just impossible,
you have no idea what he is like,
he would certainly have turned me out
and made my mother's life unbearable
if it wasn't unbearable before.
If I can describe him, he is a man
who equates permissive with diabolical.
Reading about a drug-raid once at breakfast
he threw a chair across the room
and swore till he was purple—swearing's
all right, and malt whisky, and chair-breaking,
but not sex.   I have sometimes wondered
how he got over conceiving me,
or perhaps—if he ever did get over it.
—I am sorry, this is irrelevant.
I wanted to say that I—that my actions
are not very good and I don't defend them,
but I could not have the baby,

I just could not, you do see?
And now I never want to have one,
that's what it's done to me.   I'm sick
of thinking, regretting, wishing, blaming.
I've gone so dead I see it all
like pulled from someone else's womb
and I can almost pity her
till I remember I'd be best
to forget the loss was mine.

*The Father*

Did she?   Did she?   I'm really not surprised
I'm really not.   Vodka, rum, gin—
some night yon was.   Was it me?
Was it my bairn?   Christ I don't know,
it might have been, I had her all right—
but there was three of us you know—
at least three—there was big Alec
and the wee French waiter wi the limp
(what d'ye cry him, Louie, wee Louie)—
and we went to this hut down by the loch—
it was a perfect night, perfect night—
mind you, we were all staggering a bit
but she was the worst let me tell you.
Big Alec, he's standing behind her and
kinna nibbling her neck and he leans over
and pulls her breasts out and says What have we here?
and she's giggling with her hair all over the place—
she looked that stupit we were all laughing—
no, I'm telling a lie, we werny all laughing,
I'll aye remember the French kid, Louie,
he wasny laughing, eyes like wee ferrets
as if he'd never seen yon before, and maybe
he hadn't, but he couldny take his eyes off her.

We got in the hut, into the hut
and see her, soon as we were in that door —
out like a light, flat on her back.
Well, I got going, then the other two,
but if you ask me they didny do much,
they'd had a right skinful and they were —
anyhow, I don't remember much after that,
it all goes a bit hazy.   But I do remember
coming out of the hut it was a lovely night,
it was July and it was a lovely night
with the big trees and the water an all.

*The Porter*

Ah know ah tellt them lies at the enquiry.
Ah sayed ah thought the wean wis dead
when ah took it tae the incinerator.
Ah didny think the wean wis dead,
but ah didny ken fur shair, did ah?
It's no fur me tae question the doctors.
Ah get a bag fae the sister, right?
She says take that an burn it.   She's only
passin on the doctor's instructions,
but she seen the wean, she thought it wis dead,
so ye canny blame her.   And the doctor says
ye canny blame him.   Everybody wants
tae come doon on me like a tonna bricks.
Ah canny go aboot openin disposal bags —
if ah did ah'd be a nervous wreck.
Ah passed two electricians in the corridor
and ah tellt them the wean wis alive
but they thought ah wis jokin.   Efter that
ah jist shut up, an left it tae the boilerman
tae fin oot fur hissel — he couldny miss it
could he?   The puir wee thing wis squeelin

through the bag wis it no? Ah canny see
ah had tae tell him whit was evident.
—Ah know ah'm goin on aboot this.
But suppose the kiddy could've been saved—
or suppose the boilerman hadny noticed it—
mah wee lassie's gote a hamster, ye ken?—
and ah fixed up a treadmill fur it
and it goes roon an roon an roon—
it's jist like that. Well ah'm no in court noo.
Don't answer nothin incriminatin, says the sheriff.
And that's good enough fur yours truly.
And neither ah did, neither ah did,
neither ah did, neither ah did.


## The Rainbow Knight's Confession. *Pete Morgan*

My armour *becomes* me.
I have it to the letter now—
even the colour of my steed,
a much deliberated white.

When black becomes the colour of the good
I shall ride black.
In the meantime
piebalds are for taking.

My helmet is of *catholic* proportions—
nothing fancy—just the stoutest tin
and not too loud for roustabouts to clang.

My visor's of an intricate design—
so I see out and no one else sees in.

I carry colours more than arms
but that is for the better
if there's challenge in the air.
My colours won't offend—
with rainbows there.

I change my colour for my company—
a purple knight sees purple in my cloth
a yellow knight sees yellow
blue knight blue
the blackest knights I raise my visor to.

I wear my stirrups midway
from my girth—wanting not
to offend the gentlemen of court
who tell the talents of a man
from being short on strappage
else too long, and therefore foolish—
and all of that through armour.

There is no doubt I cut a pretty rig
I am saluted more than I salute—
which is as it should be.

My breast-plate is most carefully prepared
with daily rubs of talcum and such tricks.
I make not too much noise—
with oils from Persia I have learnt
to cut out all my jangle, squeak and clank.
I hear more times than I am heard.

I have my hauberk metalled to a T
and all in all the time is going well.

Only in my private chambers
do I stand apart from this.
I place my armour in the corner then
or else I'm working on its gleam.

O sure, this armour's only implement
I mind my body too—
rub oils in that
and pare it where it grows.
I bathe it daily,
daily shave my chin.

There's nothing else except the hair of it
and I have learnt a trick or two with that—
*I comb it, where it grows, across my horns.*


## The Toft Hill Poem. *Pete Morgan*

I am the bull with the rumpus horn
My blood is bitter brine.

Only to the sky
I sing
'*I am thine*'.

I cut my colour till it runs
Yet find no root in blade and bone.

Within my head lie dark and doubt
Yet neither of these gifts I own.

I am the bull with the rumpus horn
My blood is bitter brine—
'*To whom can I ring true?*'

There is no history to tell
I sail from shade to shade
My only company this song—
This little truth I made:

'*My hide was black as ebony*
  *My eyes they were of jade*
*Across my horn in false design*
  *Were gall and wormwood laid.*'


## I think of this as something for the Sun. *Pete Morgan*

Take this tree
on which is carved a heart and several arrows
Take this pin
on the head of which is inscribed the Lord's Prayer
Take this knife
on which are written the names of the twelve apostles
Take this pomegranate.

Take the tree
and sit beneath it
Take the knife
and cut the pomegranate
Take the pin
and seed by seed, eat the fruit.

Then—when you have picked the husk quite clean—
you put away the tree
the knife, the pin
*and think of this as something for the sun.*

## In Which I Sing His Life & Times. *Pete Morgan*

Though one of his gifts
was the gift of a rose
they have accepted nothing.

Although it heralded undoubted beauty
they looked past its bloom, its fragrance
and saw only its thorn.

*Again he returned*
*bearing gifts of thistles.*

This is how they approached him—
smiling, acceptable,
holding out their fingers.

That is where they went to—
their fingers in their mouths,
their smiles fading at their body's puzzlement.

*It is from that safe distance that they sing*
*their little songs of roses, roses.*


## At Harry's Funeral. *David Morrison*

Two hundred men gathered
And walked down from the road
To the grave;
All in all, this was the funeral
Of the year.

   (I was told to be there;
   The town librarian had to attend
   The funeral of a Library Committee councillor.)

Farmers, shopkeepers, councillors,
Clerks, bankers, all were there,
Men of every age, but men born
Of this close community.

They had known Harry,
I had not;
They were born here;
I was not;
And I knew I was not one of them.

And two hundred men walked
Down the path, left, slowly right,
Left, slowly right;
There was no hurry;
Everyone seemed to have the day off
In honour of old Harry.

And they walked wearily,
Their boots heavy with some
Nervous hesitancy.

I listened to their chatter,
Around me, words forged each nail
For that coffin.

> He had a hell o a life, really.
> Hell o a guid life, I mean.

>> Hoo he managed tae spend three fortunes
>> I'll never ken.

> He's pit monie a woman tae an early grave,
> The auld bastard.

Losh, could Harry howp the whisky.
I admit that he kent weel hoo tae live,
Bit aa the destruction in his wake.

Caithness'll no be the same wi'oot him.

Ay, Harry wis a character aaricht.

And he did tak in wee Jeannie and her waen.

I'll miss his dirty jokes.
It's aboot time he wis deid.

Around me words forged
Nails of laughter, hate,
Love regret;
He was to be well nailed.

As we neared the minister
And the inevitable hypocrisy,
I knew each of the two hundred
Were aware of an unreality.

They had known Harry;
I had not.
They were born here;
I was not.

We stood, heard the ash and dust
Clatter on the seasoned wood,
The grey earth,
I knew two hundred men
Began to realise relief.

As we walked up the path,
I heard a man behind me laugh.

Wouldn't put it past the old buggar
Tae get oot o that.

At this funeral of the year

Two hundred men were seen
To almost race up the path.

Another answered.

  Ay, Harry wis aye yin fir a joke.

I turned around to meet a smile.
Twenty minutes later I was in a pub,
Learning about Harry,
Joking about Harry,
  (The old buggar I never knew.)

And I forged my nail.

## Nostalgie. *Stephen Mulrine*

Well, the George Squerr stchumers huv pit the hems
oan Toonheid's answer tae London's Thames;
thuv peyed a squaad ooty Springburn broo
tae kinfront the kinawl wi its Watterloo,
an dampt up Monklan's purlin stream
fur some dampt bailie's petrol dream,
some Tory nutter wi caurs oan the brain—
jis shows ye, canny leave nuthin alane,
the scunners.

Aye, thuv waistit Toonheid's claim tae fame;
an minny's the terrs Ah hud as a wean,
fishin fur roach aff the slevvery wa,
an pullin oot luckies, mebbe a baw,
ur a bike, even, howked up ooty the glaur;
bit thuv timmed oot the watter, fur chuckies an taur;
jis cowped the kinawl fulla slag, ten a penny,
an wheecht aw the luckies away tae the Clenny—
aye, hunners.

An thuv plankt the deid dugs aw swelt wi disease,
an pickt oot thur graves wi wee wizzent trees
tae relieve the monotony, eight tae a mile—
brek wan stick aff, thull gie ye the jile.
Ach thurs nuthin tae beat a gude pie in the sky,
bit Ah mind the kinawl easy-oasyin by,
an it isnae the same Toonheid noo at aw,
an therrs even the rats is shootin the craw—
nae wunners.

Fur thuv drapped an Emm Wan oan the auld Toonheid,
an thurs nae merr dugs gonny float by deid,
jis caurs, jis breezin alang in the breeze,
terrin the leafs aff the hauf-bilet trees,
hell-bent fur the east—(aye yir no faur wrang)
wi thur taur chuckies tae see thum alang.
Ach, nivver mind, son—they kin aw go tae hell,
an we'll jis stick, like the Monklan itsel—
non-runners.


**Diogenes.** *Stephen Mulrine*

Ah saw Diogenes the day
Rubbin frayed hauns in a doorway,
Rid-eyed, saffrin-beardit, jis stude
Therr, mummlin jeezis in wude
Alkahol; stchewed fae the skruff
Tae the burst buits, wi jis enough
Nous tae watch Billy Two Rivers destroy
Some anonymous chancer.
                    Wherrat the aul boy
Scuffled his buits in approval, sane,
It wid seem, when it comes
Tae a fast flyin merr taen
In Cuthbertson's windae, wi nae
Holds, nae barrel, nae strikcher,
Nae nuthin.   Jis pikcher.

### Record Session. *Stephen Mulrine*

Still here, the boy and girl sit,
still; the mermaid floating
on a bay of coats,
the lean Red Indian that squats
by her side.   This track
they know; I hear them talking
through their music, and walk
past.   The kitchen wall flakes
damply from my hand.
Today's analysis broke down
on stony ground;
I shut their minds;
perhaps they would not open.
The kettle boils.   I keep
returning to them.   Salt seeps
quietly from the wall.   What happens?
Are they moved to kiss,
one still, small fragment of my class?
A rotting wall makes space
between us; more than this.

## The Clyde Coast. *Robin Munro*

I'm watching
my childhood
become a development

dreaming of ships in a field, lost like seagulls.

There are roads
on the sea
to take from the tide
all the power of our world,

and Cumbrae,
an embryo,
rests in a nuclear womb.
Dunoon sinks in holy protection.

Hamburg and
Rotterdam used
to be green, some one said,
but it's long since the avocets left.

My children
will learn how
the Oil-port had islands
once touching a blue world we sailed on.

### Planting. *Robin Munro*

planting
saying with spade and
hand and cracking finger
nails
    it's worth it
I'm the way
you'll go
      it's all worth while

trees that will grow longer than my life
and trees to take and touch and love
from some one dead
who might not care for me

offering wallflower to the saddest soil
in hope of resurrection
burying the dead bird where the grass will grow
trying to mind the old man's talk
forgetting

stretching out the wrinkled soil
sifting my bit hope from stones
dug deep in rubbish
evening the order
           to affect things
faster

poems in private places of my mind
spilling heart ink just to say
I am a life
to make the permanent ink oracle
agree and give me back
my judgment
        that it's worth it

planting
praying—with a tired dry throat
and drained out unused love
like this—the way you'll go
to growing things
will justify us

repeating to the grass, the tree,
the other body, and the empty night,
you'll help me, won't you
touch me with the point
of planting.

**David.** *Robin Munro*

so david
took the sling firm in his hand
lifted five small stones and
looked straight at the
figure grey before him

and as he went to place
one stone, the giant quietly
smiled and quietly
took one small grey step
put all his weight down on the boy

where he stands
awaits approval

i imagine david
living underneath it all
still uses nail and tooth and causes
some slight irritation.

### The Baking of Bread. *Edward Borland Ramsay*

My Brother—being a baker of bread—
prepared and distributed the edible Gospel
in a lifetime of Communal Service!

His daily dozens—(those wholesome crisp-breads—
which never failed to satisfy) were symbolic
of four relevant Truths:— Seedtime, Harvest, 'Bread of Life',
and, 'The Last Supper'!

From the upper room of the Bakehouse,
the kneaded dough—in mobile ovens—still descends
by degrees, to fall in neat steps of loaves that lead
down to Dispatch!

Like us, they are all shapes and sizes!
Their colour may be different too!—some White, some Brown—
others no doubt, with a darker crust!   Some may even
be shan*; but there is a use for them all!—
In one way, or another, they wait to be broken
for our necessity!

We are all valuable products of God's great oven!

* *Bakers' term for badly shaped loaves.*

## Brown Owl. *Edward Borland Ramsay*

Fuzz-faced, and, looking like a hank of wool,
the Brown Owl sits on the grey branch—
waiting perhaps, for the field-mouse or bank-vole
to tempt him from his prudent perch!
Dusk will unravel his drowsy wits,
and let him down on unsuspecting prey!
Being Predator, his nocturnal sallies are
macabre! He will gorge himself—
(when the Rodent cycle is complete)
till tails hang from his beak like the roots
of grotesque plants! He seldom recants!—
but whits! and flits with moonlit eyes
in search of future sustenance!
He is a wise creature!—he knows when and where
the cycle will be repeated! He is caught up
in the Spinning-wheel of existence—a quaint pattern
of Nature's handiwork!


## It Seems so Strange. *Edward Borland Ramsay*

It seems so strange—
the simple chores we do:—
    The setting of a plate for instance,
upon a late-night table;—
a saucer, with an inverted cup—
(this, to keep it clean, in preparation
for early morning tea!)

I remember going
to my father's house one morning—
and finding him dead!   The table
had been set for his solitary need:
In the coal-cellar, I found
a pathetic little bundle
of dried twigs; some twists of paper and,
a scuttleful of small coals:—
It seemed so strange, to see the last signs
of habitation, in that deserted house!


**The Washing of Hands.** *Edward Borland Ramsay*

The symbolic Action—
committed under an admonitory flow
of liquid language, or, in a still-life basin—
has unique significance!

For my own part,
I prefer to wash my hands
in running water!   In that way,
I am less conscious of the day's
contamination!   I am not confronted
with the concentrate of my own uncleanliness!

In our daily ordinance,
we have all been guilty of static compunction!—
We consider our own perplexed images, and,
like Pontius Pilate, turn to our ablution!
Would to God, we were more conscious of
'The Cleansing Blood of Christ'.

### The Parade of the Skirts. *Osmond Robb*

The skirts of the well-groomed matrons
Were patterned with big squares
Dividing the russet or the dull green cloth
Like barren ground new-surveyed but unloved.
Then came swaying, lifting, filling,
A dark wide skirt all star-flowered
Like the fields of heaven.
My inward sight still pastures there.

### A last word to Sharon before bed. *Douglas Rome*

As you tiptoe out of bed, slip
through the beckoning mirror
into your real nursery,
glide to the stars on the moon's prow;
remember to pay the toll
to the guardians—forty golden
winks they demand—or they'll slide the
black door shut behind you and
hold you hostage against
the breaking of the dawn.

## Report from the Asylum. *Douglas Rome*

1. *A walk in the sun.*

Blood flowers
quicker than
a rose said
the patient
to the man
tending the
hospital
garden.   The
gardener
said nothing,
bent closer
to the buds,
willing a
quick season
through the soil.

2. *Guy Fawkes boy.*

Stuffed into a wheelchair,
lolling, boneless, pushed everywhere
like a Fawkes Night straw man;
pupils swimming out of his
head (a really hopeless case).

But at nights in the
ward, after an injection to blunt the
stabbing peak of his fit, he sleeps;
orders the movement
of his chair as others
order the movement of their limbs.

And, as he rides,
the rims of the big round
wheels glow red,
the silver spokes
flash and whirr
like catherine wheels
in November.

3. *Doctor's notebook.*

'No-one saw it flap over
the horizon, but the sky
was suddenly soundless and
clouds of starlings fell to earth
like rain.   The air quivered.   Then
stillness.   The big bird with the
chipped beak wheeled in the sun and
as its shadow blanketed
the field I stood scarecrow-stiff,
eyes trembling.   It worked.   I felt
the shadow passing.   Movement—
any movement at all—would
have tugged the great beak through me.'

4. *The man in the locked ward.*

In this room he
learned to be neutral
as the water
in the glass.   He learned
to efface himself
so well that the
mirror barely
registered his
presence.   Each day as

the water in the
glass diminished
his perception
of himself shrank.

The last time he
looked in the mirror
he saw nothing but
the glass.   Empty.


**Greek Fire.**   *Alexander Scott*

GREEK FIRE

*Delphi*

Castalian water,
clearest of every
spring,
cleanse my
imagination,
even as you cleanse my
mouth,
and make me sing like the
sybil
from the navel-stone of the
world,
with the voice of
inspiration,
the terrible edge of
truth,
and all the ambiguities of
art.

JOURNEY AND PLACE

To ride into a myth
and find it real,
yet more fantastic than the most
fabulous dream.

This is the legend
shaped in a land,
this is the country
formed in a fable.

THORN PHILOSOPHY

*Athens*

Trod on a
thorn
in the Theatre of Dionysus
and didn't give a
single
howling curse
that its ultimate
umpteenth
great–great–grandpappy thorn
might once have had the pricking
privilege
to sting the Socratic
sole.

PAST AND PRESENT

*Saronic shore*

Guide said
'Piraeus
long walls
Spartans
disaster'

Guide said
'Salamis
wooden walls
Persians
victory'

Saw them through a fun-fair.

ARCADY

The shepherds of Arcadia
look like lumberjacks
and herd goats.

The goats are glossy brown
and horned, like the
county of Arcadia,
the landscape lion's hide
and horned with mountains.

The goats have the face of Pan,
the antique mask of
an outlook older than men,
and other—

The otherworld of
Arcadia.

## STADIUM AND TAVERNA

*Olympia*

Zeus and Hera
are dead rubble
where runners sprinted
for olive crowns.

But Dionysus and Pan
(with ouzo and bouzouki)
achieve the eternal
revel.

## NOBLE SPLENDOUR

*Thessaly*

Two white horses.
One green field.

## MOUNTAIN MONASTERIES

*Meteora*

Up and down
precipitous cliffs
in a rope basket
only changed when the
rope broke.

Contempt for the flesh
a faith that faced a
fall
of
three
hundred
feet.

### SARONIC GULF

Crossed to Aegina
halfseasover.

### DARLING

And Sappho
too
was 'small
and dark'

—a dagger
of love.

### LOVE IN AEGINA

As I
entered,
the shrilling
cicadas
shrieked to
silence.

### BAD TASTE

They say that Socrates drank.
He took hemlock.

Anything, anything
rather than *retsina*.

### DIFFERENCE

Centaur
stencilled on cabin wall.

She said,
'Neither man nor beast,'

He said,
'Man and animal both.'

Torso human,
quarters horse.

But joined
exactly
*where?*

### GOLDEN MYCENAE

Stones and graves,
stones and graves,
the haunt of heroes,
the hell of slaves,
with never a glint
of their golden glaives,
their glittering fetters,
their gleaming staves,
but ruin, ruin,
stones and graves.

AGORA

*Corinth*

Roman Corinth leaves me cold
even in the blaze of noon,
although St Paul stood preaching here,
then kept in touch by letter
on faith and hope and love.

This market-place shows faith
in market-values only,
the hope of gain,
the love of profit.

A dull huddle of cheap stones,
a couple of facing platforms, equally mean,
the one where the saint spoke,
the other where slaves were auctioned.

Whose voice was louder,
the auctioneer's or the apostle's?

And whose is louder now?

MELTEMI

*North wind, Aegina*

Darkness and sleep have lost the struggle
with wind and sea,
the wind flogging the waves
to charge and charge and charge and charge
the rocky shoreline,
butting and goring.

Now I know why
Poseidon,
god of the great waters,
was Earth-Shaker,
Bull from the Sea.

Out of the depths I hear him
bellowing anger,
trampling, trampling.

The earth shudders,
the air of the island quakes.

ACCOMPANIMENT

*Aegina*

In the day
   the cicadas
      scissor the light.

In the dark
   the seaserpent
      hisses the night.

HOTEL GARDEN

*Aegina*

Roses
from hoses
to mock
the rock.

LAST MORNING

*Aegina*

Eve she excelled,
she brought me figs
from the wild fig-tree
and shining grapes
from the tentless vine.

ORACULAR

Awake all night in the cauldron of summer Athens,
listening all night long
to the brangle of engines, the squeal of brakes,
the screech of tormented tyres,
aware that these noises assaulting the nerves
are an agonised image
of twentieth-century time,
I think on the silence of Delphi,
Parnassus brooding
above a grey-green ocean of olives,
a double million drowsing their still dream,
but also remember
that even there, at the temple of reason,
the shrine of the human spirit
(where bright Apollo
uttered his dark oracles from doped mouths),
the priests accused old Aesop,
the fabulist of reason,
and hurled him down to death from the Shining Rocks
as a sacrilegious telltale,
an emblematic ending
for every tongue to truth.

BETWEEN DELPHI AND THEBES

Where Swollenfoot once did his daddy in
   (Where Oedipus slew his sire)
The bauxite mines have swollen, 'grey as tin,'
   To dowse the Muse's fire.

But still she blazes song in the dark dale
   That drives from Delphi down,
Her flame a radiance wrenched from ash and shale
   Where every light should drown.

She sings of wine and oil from the sterile shade
   Where even the grass is grey,
Of riches dredged from dearth, the dreary glade
   A glitter to wealth's way.

The road runs through, but still the riddling Sphinx
   Demands reply, reply,
'If plenty thrives from greater gloom, who thinks
   Of legend lore?   And why?'

The road runs through to Thebes, its twists and turns
   A maze that mirrors thought
To teach the truth that every traveller learns,
   Though scarce the truth he sought.

The Sphinx is male and female, close conjoint,
   And all its riddles tricks,
And every crossroads stands at the still point
   Where light and darkness mix.

## Collected Cargo. *Alexander Scott*
For George Bruce's *Collected Poems* 39/70

In the bad times
when fighters pounced from sun to sea
with guns aglitter as wave-dazzle

and in these better times
when only the sea was the callous killer
of men who went down in ships

you trawled for the silver darlings
with words in nice nets
that lured them shining into your hold

from a sea too chill for story
to a land too plain for myth,
your fishing fathomed full of its own legend.


## Russian Poem. *Iain Crichton Smith*

1. Sometimes one feels like Chekhov, waiting for something to happen,
   for the Revolution to happen, for the glasses all to break
   and the pear-bellied merchants to shake on their cushions,
   and the troikas to disappear into an arena of dust.
   Melancholy man, he felt the future in his soul,
   and it quivered in obsolete gardens with a white light,
   it settled on the powdered shoulders of bankrupt women.
   Troikas, samovars, versts, how beautiful they seem,
   how remote these conversations in theatrical mansions
   and the light of the Russian sky, part of the scenery.

The brown peasants leaned on their rakes with vacant eyes,
thick lips, and the thick necks of the past,
they peered into the windows as at a sweet shop,
their scythes waved in the evening as if asking questions.
The willowy people conversed, and the peasants waited.
And the sisters waited in the provincial houses
dusting the wardrobes, the dressers, dying of ennui,
dreaming of Moscow, St Petersburg, the handsome cavalry,
binoculars in boxes, parasols by the Black Sea.
Ah, Chekhov, consumptive of the spirit,
instinctive diagnostic of terror, your patient was Russia,
it was restless, dying, turning over and over in its dying,
clamouring for water, milk, for the fever of vodka.
It was wanting to die, it was wanting to be renewed,
it was wanting its iron, its mineral armour again,
it was finished with the bankrupt nobles and its dreaming Hamlets,
it wanted its Fortinbras to fling the red curtains wide.

2. Ivanov, to marry your Sonia was tempting,
   to marry the young girl in her innocence and dew,
   to leave your wardrobes like upright coffins in the dust
   and your house which resounded with uncles and hysteria.
   It seemed a solution, a perfect gift from Heaven,
   to recover your innocence in the newness of white sheets,
   to listen to the hum of the cooker in the morning,
   and to see your Sonia, her arms white with flour.
   But it was impossible, the Idea was against it,
   the aimless procession of people and the seasons,
   the perfectly groomed skulls nibbling at the salt herring,
   and dipping their fingers into the cherry preserves.
   There was no end to the card games and the bingo,
   the abolition of art, the fattening of the spirit,
   the meaningless acres roasting under the sun,
   the illiteracy, the boredom, the garrulous dummies.

Ah, the sky was not innocent enough,
it had washed too many pastures like an old rag
it was worn out, it had lost its colour.
Ivanov, you saw it would not do,
you raised the revolver till you could see it in the mirror
and a shot rang out like the Neva breaking its ice.

3. And then there was you Tolstoy aristocrat of the body
who challenged the Westernist Turgenev to a duel
unable to tolerate the kind of talent he had.
You also as a child jumped out of the window
to prove that like a young Mercury you could fly.
But the body was not enough, there was something missing,
the spirit made its demands on the cavalryman
the lynx-eyed Homer had his way to go.
The spirit eats the artist at the end,
the hate of Lear, who was himself a Lear.
who went out into the storm to die at a railway station
maddened by book-keeping and hero worship.
It was impossible for you to become a saint,
you were too infatuated with objects,
with houses, people, Russia, Napoleon,
archetype of the amoral opaline conman.
The bearded god died in the smoke of trains,
the rural man in the fire and light of the city.
No, it wasn't enough, the world of the New Testament,
the impeccable light of the willowy yellow man
walking always by the azure and depth of the sea.
Your contempt for art was real, but your love of angels
unreal, untypical.   I see you repairing your boots
while Russia turns over in its immense sleep
and the angels are red descending over your acres
where at one time your boots were polished and tall
in the mirror where the Cossacks ran riot,
and heaven was a globe that rested like a hawk on your hand.

4. Dostoevski, you taught us the power of humiliation,
   the kneeling of the spirit at the confessional.
   The idiot and the saint walk in an urban light
   and tuberculosis is the plague from which all suffer.
   The underground man survives in his clear madness
   as you yourself survived in that prison
   to which you were exiled for a minor pamphlet.
   Let the Tsar be defeated by the weeping soul,
   by the genuflexion of weakness,
   let the posse of internal police follow the student
   to where he has buried evidence of his crime.
   After all we aren't as mad as Nietzsche
   whose scholarly soul was entranced by violence.
   After all, the chains can't be severed.
   The meek shall inherit the earth.
   Though he should gauchely walk in the light of plagues and brothels
   he is, like the artist, perfect in heaven,
   though he should flare garishly in worldly mansions
   he comes home at last in perfect obedience
   to the slavery endemic in his nature.
   You and the aristocrat never met—
   like the North and the South Pole you respected each other—
   and you arrived at a similar place
   where the head was bowed at Gennasareth
   lolling on the cross, staring far beyond Rome.


*Lenin*

5. So you came and everything exploded.
   The liberal man believed in discreet dosages
   for an old patient who was becoming violent
   and throwing the icons out into the snow.
   It was snowing—was it snowing when you came?
   After Europe to be home again.
   After conspiracies with cardboard men,
   Plekhanov, theoreticians of nothing.

To breathe the air of Russia again!
You in your cap looking like a minor
railway official in a brown painting
or even a comic man in the silent films.
And you were really a mine ticking away,
your head was round and solid like a mine.
You listened angrily to the moony speeches,
like a farmer who has work to do,
who sees the dawn rising and is impatient,
your hands resting on your knees, about to get up
to drive Russia along like a huge cow.
And then you stood up and said 'War,
Nothing but war, no compromise.'
Your will was inflexible (though you were often sick,
or so one has read, in great crises)
You looked as if you were made of stone.
You sounded like a voice from the future.
It was the end of ennui, the beginning of cannon.
A great shapeless hulk began to stir—
Russia in the snow and in the shadow.
You were the squat captain at the prow
directing operations, barking orders,
signing papers in a perpetual hailstorm,
running from window to window with your intelligence,
banging down philosophies like stamps,
forging each day like an iron coin.
Switzerland and England, how far away!
These days of being a tramp of the imagination!
Now every motion was approved by Marx,
he was your Moses of St Petersburg.
Behind the newsprint was Das Kapital
as a large landscape behind driving snow

And the writers wrote for you.   Mayakovsky
left his ladder of images and came to you
till his ladder which had flickered became stone,
and he killed himself, really! for something personal—
'the boat had smashed on the rocks'.   Imagine that!
Mayakovsky could afford to kill himself for love!
What a ridiculous notion!   How juvenile!
To think of roses at a time like this!
—when statistics were unfavourable, when the night
sang with a high pure lunacy, this country
which had no right to exist, delicately trembling
under the constellations, one drop of dew.

But the dead looked at you from a far horizon
before the lid was shut on them, and they descended
into the necessary well of the Idea!
'Let them eat each other, let them be thrown down,
let them eat each other, as in Maupassant's story
of the dogs they threw down a well in France
and the strongest of them survived in the darkness.
This country is a hallucination, a flash of lightning,
a vision—hardly more than that,
with hob-nailed booted men trembling in transition,
There is no time.   Take that hand away.
My head has become square like a book on sewage.
My room is a tank.   Let me have that gun.
Blow the Salvation Army out of Russia!
I want engineers.   What is Tolstoy to me.
Then lovers, what are they doing there?   They should be working.
Spring?   By my skull-shaped watch it is midnight.
I've had nothing for years but the sound of my own mind. . .
and the millions of people who consult me, endlessly,
Dr Lenin, Consultant to the Revolution.
Ah, Russia, how I love you.   But—abolish uncles,
aunts, parties, stupid Ivanovs.

Gogol was funny.   But he had icy glasses,
twinkling down the avenues of humour.
There is no time for humour, it is a bourgeois concept,
designed as protection from reality.
As for us, let there be no protection,
let us see further than heaven itself!
We will cut Russia to the very bone.
I will carry her on my back if necessary.
But it is so silent.   Sometimes in this room
I also feel the attraction of suicide,
but I haven't the time to raise the gun to my head.'


**Everything is silent.** *Iain Crichton Smith*

Everything is silent now
before the storm.
The transparent walls tremble.
You can hear the very slightest hum
of a stream miles away.

The silence educates your ear.
The threat is palpable.
You can hear the boots behind the mountains.
You can hear the breathings of feathers.
You can hear the well of your heart.

You know what it is that permits the walls,
that allows the ceiling,
that lets the skin cling to your body,
that mounts the spiral
of your beholden bones.

That sorrow is a great sorrow
and leaves you radiant
when the tempest has passed
and your vases are still standing
and your bones are stalks in the water.


**Early Films.** *Iain Crichton Smith*

From the cinema these voices return,
these early arias
which are like fire over stone.
Don't you remember

how towards these smoky screens
youth stared with wild eyes?
The organist picked out in marble,
the plush carpets,
houses such as we never owned,
the closest we came to
villas of the wide-armed farewells,
the crumpling faces.

Ah, how it all returns.    The piano
played in the house by the cliff,
the demented lady dying in music,
the velvety water,
and the chipped angels blowing their trumpets
from a peeling ceiling.

It was the closest we came to
the spaciousness that was to die
down the great stairways
in the glasses that tinkled
just before the bell tolled
and the lion mouthed and snarled.

## Takes on the Crash. *Roderick Watson*

At the point where the wheel stops
spinning in the ditch    and the last drop
of water on the wire    drops down
to shattered safety glass:    say          Jesus Christ!
'I hated myself as never before'      You should see us go
in the car's slow roll to the verge      upside down
shedding skins on dry grass         across the road!
(lights and wing-mirrors flying
your swimsuit was found 100 yards away
and the bushes were growing sandwiches)
later we would laugh at a story for parties.

'Things really do slow down' I said
at the point where the wheel stops
spinning in the ditch    and the last drop
of blood blackens the grass    held still      —I'm sorry
for fear of moving    without speech for fear    God I'm sorry
of losing breath    with a life so frail      God I'm sorry
and brittle;    and problems like getting home    I'm sorry.
now    and how the tar is squeezed out
on the edge of the road    picked up
and rolled to a dusty ball    in the summer
when it's hot    it runs . . .

to the point where the wheel stops
responding to the will    and the slow trees
push in their leaves and branches
to the mind    and your damp hair      —crush the engine
on the beach    with the cut of elastic      to your breast
on your skin after the picnic:    the day    and fold us up
so white around us    sea light      like sheets.
and sand on the brown of your legs
as gulls shriek into the sun
at the point where the heart stops
spinning in the ditch    and the last drop
of water on the wire    drops down.

## Tutorial. *Heather Wood*

He runs long white fingers
Through long fair hair
And says 'Oh gosh, oh father'.
He straightens large spectacles
On his long thin nose
And says 'Oh, I dunno'.

His long legs twine
Round the front of the desk,
The whole tutorial memorises
The pattern of his socks,
And forgets to notice
The influences on foreign policy.

Again he modestly denies
That he is an expert,
He is doing a Ph.D.
On an entirely different period,
With that nervous laugh he recommends
We ask Dr Neverin, actually.

The long long scarf is there
On the back of the door,
Just like it was last week,
And there is his stapler,
Soon he will pick it up
And play with it: The Firmagrip.

His shoes still need polishing,
And the paperback on The Marxist View
Is still on the desk,
His long large friendly grin
Is still, I dunno actually,
Feebly doing its best, you know.

# SCOTTISH POETRY 6

© Edinburgh University Press
22 George Square, Edinburgh

*North America*
Aldine · Atherton, Inc.

Printed in Great Britain by
W & J Mackay Limited, Chatham

The Publishers gratefully acknowledge
permission to reprint *The Auld Symie*
by Jake Flower, given by Mr Duncan
Glen, and the poems by David McDuff,
from *Words in Nature* (Ramsay Head
Press, Edinburgh).